Dearest Malcolm

May you *know* win
any 'F1 only charity quiz".

Happy Reading in 2012

love . hugs

Angela

FORMULA ONE
On This Day

FORMULA ONE
On This Day

History, Facts & Figures
from Every Day of the Year

ROB BURNETT

FORMULA ONE
On This Day

History, Facts & Figures from Every Day of the Year

All statistics, facts and figures are correct as of 1st July 2009

© Rob Burnett

Rob Burnett have asserted their rights in accordance with the Copyright, Designs and Patents Act 1988 to be identified as the authors of this work.

Published By:
Pitch Publishing (Brighton) Ltd
A2 Yeoman Gate
Yeoman Way
Durrington
BN13 3QZ

Email: info@pitchpublishing.co.uk
Web: www.pitchpublishing.co.uk

First published 2009

A catalogue record for this book is available from the British Library.

10-digit ISBN: 1-9054116-3-4
13-digit ISBN: 978-1-9054116-3-4

Printed and bound in Malta by Gutenberg Press

INTRODUCTION

There have been 30 World Champions since F1 began in 1950, more than one hundred race winners, and 25 winning constructors.

But as ever, the statistics don't tell you the whole story. What I've tried to do in this book is look at some of the quirky or unusual events in the sport that flesh it out and make it more than just another racing series.

As with most sports, F1 is about the personalities as much as the racing and the exploits of the protagonists both on and off the track is what keeps us all hooked.

Some of my favourite tales include Alberto Ascari taking an unplanned dip in the Monaco harbour along with his Lancia during the 1955 race, Taki Inoue tangling with the course marshal's car, and Nigel Mansell's unlikely first win for Ferrari.

Of course, as one of the most dangerous sports in the world, F1 has had more than it's share of tragedies, and many of the stories in this book are not happy ones, but those drivers who lost their lives racing for our entertainment deserve to be remembered.

Writing this book has given me a great excuse to spend hours and hours poring over books, reading old race reports and watching old races to gather material – never has 'work' been so much fun and I hope that reading each little morsel of history I have found is as enjoyable as it was pulling them all together.

Rob Burnett, August 2009

FORMULA ONE
On This Day

JANUARY

JANUARY 1

While New Year's Day is traditionally for nursing a hangover and trying to remember your ambitious resolutions, for a few years in the sixties it was also when the F1 season started with the South African Grand Prix. Jim Clark won in 1965 on his way to his second World Championship and he also triumphed in 1968 at Kyalami. It was an historic victory as it took Clark to 25 race wins – the most in the history of the sport and one more than Fangio, whose record had stood for ten years. Tragically it was not only Clark's last win, but also his last championship race as he was killed in a crash at the Hockenheimring in Germany four months later.

Some of motor racing's finest have been recognised by the Queen on this day in the New Year's Honours list. Jack Brabham and Frank Williams both became knights today in 1979 and 1999 respectively.

JANUARY 2

Nigel Mansell reckoned the support from his home crowd was worth a second per lap at Silverstone, which perhaps accounts for the remarkable performance of the delightfully named John Love in the South African GP at Kyalami today in 1967. He was actually from neighbouring Zimbabwe (then Southern Rhodesia). Not a regular on the F1 circuit, 42-year-old Love qualified fifth and with just seven laps to go was pulling away in the lead in his privately entered ex-Bruce McLaren Cooper. A fuel pump problem forced him to pit, robbing him of the chance to become the first African grand prix winner.

Love eventually finished second to Mexican driver Pedro Rodriguez – it was his first F1 victory in only his ninth race. While his winning streak had just begun, another was ending – it was the last win for the pioneering Cooper team, which had powered Jack Brabham to the World Championship in 1959 and 1960, the first time a rear-engined car had achieved the feat.

JANUARY 3

The first known use of the word 'automobile' was printed in a *New York Times* article on this day in 1899.

In the sixties and seventies Jackie Stewart was one of the best racing drivers in the world, but in the fifties he was not even the best in his family. The man who would go on to become a three-time World Champion was preceded in the sport by his older brother Jimmy, who made his F1 debut in the British Grand Prix at Silverstone in 1953. He retired from driving two years later after a big crash and thereafter supported his younger brother's efforts. James Robert Stewart died on this day in 2008 aged 76. In his autobiography Jackie Stewart says of his brother: 'What do I owe Jim? I owe him almost everything.'

JANUARY 4

Always on the look out for a new way of promoting his team, Eddie Jordan announced today in 2001 that his eponymous team would be entering the Honda Formula 4-stroke powerboat race series. Eddie was in typically ebullient mood when he announced the news: 'Not only does it give us a great opportunity to work with Honda on exciting projects outside Formula One, but it also provides a fast, fun and exciting environment in which to promote the Jordan name.'

Today in 2008 former Ferrari team principal Jean Todt revealed that Michael Schumacher had been offered the chance to take over running the team but had declined. 'He would have been the best candidate for this job, but he did not want it,' he said. Later Schumi added: 'When I saw how much passion and dedication that he put into his job – similar to what I did in my job – but he simply was just sitting in Maranello, day by day, even on weekends, late into night – I said: "Do I need this? Simply not. Simply not."'

JANUARY 5

The Jordan team was in the news again today in 2004 when *The Sun* newspaper reported that Russian billionaire Roman Abramovich wanted to buy the Silverstone based outfit, under the headline 'Formula Oneski for Roman'. The paper claimed he had already had four secret meetings with Eddie Jordan about buying the team and was ready to invest millions to make it successful, as he had done at Chelsea Football Club.

The following day the story was killed by a spokesman for Sibneft, one of the companies belonging to the Russian. John Mann told the Michelin F1 website: 'It is true that Roman enjoys Formula One and has met Eddie several times, but that is it. Roman has also met with Bernie Ecclestone but that doesn't mean he's going to buy his house. We just want to lay all these rumours to rest.'

JANUARY 6

The fans of Ferrari are legendary for their fanaticism and it was revealed today in 2000 how one offered to help Eddie Irvine win the 1999 World Championship by sabotaging Mika Hakkinen's car. *The Sun* newspaper claimed the fan sent Irvine a letter saying: 'My idea is I shoot a small bullet in the tyre from Mercedes and the tyre bursts and tears to pieces. Nobody can prove the shoot. Hakkinen doesn't make the finish. Would you be interested?' The threat was never carried out and Hakkinen beat Irvine to the crown.

Unlike most top-level sports, motorsport has not had a history of drug scandals but a story emerged in late 2004 when a former Ferrari team doctor named Benigno Bartoletti was quoted by Italian magazine *Quattroruote* as saying 'At races, there is a lot of cocaine and in Formula One, it could be as many as one third of all drivers who take cocaine.' Today in 2005 the FIA issued a statement rubbishing the story and said no driver had ever failed one of its drugs tests. Benigno later claimed he had been misquoted by the magazine.

JANUARY 7

When Austrian drinks company Red Bull purchased the Jaguar F1 team from Ford in 2004 it was claimed at first that they would keep the team's management in place. Today in 2005 however Tony Purnell and David Pitchforth who had been running the outfit for Ford were sacked, and replaced by Christian Horner as team principal and Gunther Steiner as technical director.

McLaren has always been a more stable outfit than most teams in the pitlane and today in 2008 the team launched the MP4/23 – the car that Lewis Hamilton drove to win the 2008 World Championship. After missing out on the 2007 title by just one point, Hamilton insisted he was ready to challenge again. He said: 'I've recovered from it and I feel even stronger, mentally and physically, and now I'm just excited and even more determined than I have been in the past. Last year was a steep learning curve. This year, I feel more at home, more confident and more relaxed, and even more sure of what I want. I honestly believe I can do an even better job this season.'

JANUARY 8

Bernie Ecclestone surprised everyone in 2008 when he announced that Donington Park had usurped Silverstone as the home of the British GP from 2010. Today in 2009 the track secured the planning permission needed to bring the circuit up to standard.

On the same day Prodrive boss David Richards ruled himself out as a potential buyer of the Honda Racing team. The squad was put up for sale in December 2008 and Richards had run the team for three years under its previous guise, BAR. 'It has also got to be financially viable,' he said. 'You expect to (have to) invest but you also expect it to work. I just personally feel that the current environment is too unsettled.'

JANUARY 9

The ultimate aim for any new Formula One team is to win races but usually it takes at least a few seasons for any new outfit to get up to speed. Today in 1977 at the Argentina Grand Prix the Walter Wolf Racing team won its very first race with Jody Scheckter behind the wheel. The team was new in name but had grown out of Frank Williams' first attempt at F1 and been renamed after Canadian millionaire Walter Wolf had purchased it and Williams had left. Scheckter started only 10th on the grid and was fortunate that six runners in front of him retired but it was still a great start for the Wolf team.

Michael Schumacher may have broken all the records in F1 but he was helped by the fact that he never had to fight his teammates who were employed simply to help him win – often to the disgust of racing fans. He retired in 2006 and today in 2007 Ferrari team boss Jean Todt told the Italian media that his drivers Kimi Raikkonen and Felipe Massa would be treated equally. 'It will be healthy if the two drivers compete against each other,' Todt said.

JANUARY 10

Two veteran drivers were proving experience is a valued commodity in F1 on this day. First off in 2003 Dutch racer Jos 'the Boss' Verstappen was confirmed as Justin Wilson's partner for the season at Minardi.

Five years later Giancarlo Fisichella was also announced at a new team. Now one of the most experienced drivers in the paddock and a member of the exclusive 200 club for drivers who have competed in more than 200 grands prix, the Italian has always been viewed as a quick driver who perhaps lacks the consistency to put together a serious tilt at the title over a whole season. Today in 2008 Fisi was announced as lead driver for the newly re-branded Force India team. It was his third stint with the team formerly known as Jordan.

JANUARY 11

A number of teams including McLaren and Minardi have built two-seater F1 cars over the years, designed to give passengers the chance to be scared witless by taking a ride with a Formula One driver. Today in 2001 Arrows went one better when they launched a three-seater version of their F1 racer. Arrows head of marketing Steve Hood said: 'By sitting slightly to the side, passengers will have a totally uncompromised view of the track ahead, which is what a driver sees. So they can see corners coming up and think, "Hang on, didn't we pass what would be a sensible braking point 100 metres ago?"'

Today in 2005 another team was due to launch their one-seater challenger for the new season. The Sauber team decided to cancel their launch, scheduled to take place on this day in the Malaysian capital Kuala Lumpur, because of the tsunami disaster that had affected the whole region. The event was designed to celebrate 10 years of F1 involvement for Sauber's Malaysian sponsor Petronas but a team spokesman said: 'As a mark of respect to the victims of the disaster in South East Asia and their families, it was decided to cancel the launch.'

JANUARY 12

Double World Champion Emerson Fittipaldi got his 1975 season off to a flier today in 1975 when he took victory at the Argentine Grand Prix. The Brazilian ace started from fifth on the grid but battled past a host of other drivers including local hero Carlos Reutemann to take the chequered flag ahead of James Hunt in second and Reutemann in third.

It was an altogether different story for Emerson's elder brother Wilson who was racing for his own team. On lap 12 his brand new car spun out of control, crashed into a barrier and caught fire. Wilson was able to get out but the car was destroyed in the blaze.

JANUARY 13

Alan Jones became the first man to win the World Championship with the Williams team in 1980. On this day that year he got his season off to the best possible start by taking victory in the Argentine Grand Prix. Also on the grid was Alain Prost who finished sixth on his F1 debut in a McLaren.

When Niki Lauda became Jaguar team boss in 2001 he was critical of modern F1 cars and claimed that even a monkey could drive a car with traction control and electronic aids. Today in 2002 he might have been regretting those words when he got behind the wheel of the Jaguar R3 at a test. After spinning twice in his first three laps he had to be towed back to the pits. The triple World Champion said: 'Yes, I have said that any monkey can drive a car nowadays, but I am simply comparing it to the driving 17 years ago. I will not make this a regular appearance. If I want to make it regular I have to train and I am not prepared to do that. For this test I didn't train, I just smoked less!'

JANUARY 14

Ferrari began a new era on this day in 2007 when the team unveiled the F2007 car at their Maranello base. The car was the first for 11 years that would not be driven by Michael Schumacher after the German had hung up his helmet at the end of the previous season.

The team need not have worried about being without the old master, as Finn Kimi Raikkonen drove the car to his first World Championship title in his first season with the Scuderia. With Felipe Massa in the second car, the F2007 also won the constructors' title – the first for Ferrari since 2004.

JANUARY 15

With the brilliant and innovative Colin Chapman at the helm the Lotus team was always a force to be reckoned with and today in 1978 Mario Andretti put in a dominant performance in the opening round of the season, the Argentine Grand Prix at Buenos Aires. The American driver put his Lotus 78 on pole and then completed a flag-to-flag victory. Andretti went on to win the drivers' title that season, while Lotus won the Constructors'. It was the last time Lotus won either championship.

Eighteen years later to the day and Team Lotus was finished. The team never really recovered from the death of founder Colin Chapman in 1982 and a gradual decline was finally ended today in 1996 when the last remnants of the business, Team Lotus Holdings Ltd, was wound up by the High Court in London.

JANUARY 16

Today in 1955 the grid lined up for the Argentine Grand Prix. Juan Manuel Fangio won the race to delight his home crowd but the meeting is more noteworthy as the hottest Grand Prix ever (since matched by the 1984 United States GP and the 2005 Bahrain GP). Temperatures were over 100°F or around 40°C and only two drivers, one of them Fangio, made it to the finish without having to hand over to a reserve driver.

Since taking over the McLaren team in 1980 Ron Dennis has been a major figure in the sport. He led the team back to winning ways while Alain Prost, Ayrton Senna, Mika Hakkinen, Niki Lauda and Lewis Hamilton have all become World Champions at the wheel of his cars. Today in 2009, at the launch of McLaren's new car, Ron announced he was to stand down as McLaren team principal before the new season began, to work on other areas of the McLaren business. 'This is very definitely not retirement,' he said. 'In fact, I intend to work even harder from now on.'

JANUARY 17

The 1954 Argentine Grand Prix was held on this day in Buenos Aires and home-grown hero Fangio took the win but it was not without controversy. He stopped on lap 61 for a tyre change and was passed by the Ferraris of Giuseppe Farina and Froilan Gonzalez. The Ferrari team manager Nello Ugolini decided to protest that Maserati had used too many mechanics to work on Fangio's car and, confident Fangio would be disqualified, he ordered his drivers to back off and take no risks. Fangio went back out and caught and passed them both to win. Ugolini was left distraught after his protest was thrown out by the stewards and the FIA, and Fangio was allowed to keep the win.

It was Fangio's first victory on home soil and the first of four consecutive wins in the Argentine Grand Prix.

JANUARY 18

The first ever Argentine Grand Prix was held today in 1953. A brainchild of President Juan Perón designed to capitalize on Fangio's success, the race was free to enter and far too many people turned up to the point where they were lining the race track. At one point Giuseppe Farina had to swerve to avoid hitting a spectator on the circuit but he lost control and crashed into the crowd. Estimates of fatalities vary from between one to 13. Alberto Ascari took the win on his way to his second World Championship.

Today in 2008 the McLaren team announced that Lewis Hamilton had signed an improved five-year deal to stay with the team, designed to reward his strong performances in his debut season when he came so close to winning the championship. Team boss Ron Dennis said: 'The announcement will take the length of our relationship with Lewis to a total of 15 years, which we believe is among the longest running associations between a sportsman and a team in the history of sport, particularly motorsport.'

JANUARY 19

The Argentine Grand Prix held today in 1958 was notable because home-grown hero Juan Manuel Fangio didn't win after taking four wins from the previous four races held in Buenos Aires. Stirling Moss took the victory in the tiny Cooper-Climax 43 entered by Rob Walker. The win was significant as it was the first in the World Championship for Cooper and the first for a rear-engined car since the Auto Unions of the 1930s. All the other teams would slowly start to catch on to the concept until it became the norm.

Bruce McLaren made his grand prix debut later in the 1958 season and today in 2007 it was announced that a film was to be made about the life of the New Zealand driver. Barrie Osborne, who had previously worked on *Apocalypse Now, The Matrix* and the *Lord of the Rings* trilogy, was signed up to produce.

JANUARY 20

For nearly 30 years the first man on the scene of any accident in Formula One was Professor Sid Watkins. Known simply as 'Prof' in the paddock, Watkins was appointed as F1's official doctor in 1978 by Bernie Ecclestone and since then he has done more than any other individual to make the sport safer. He was the man who attended to Ayrton Senna as he lay dying on the track at Imola, and it is thanks to Watkins' trackside treatment that Mika Hakkinen survived his horrific crash at Adelaide in 1995. Today in 2005 Watkins announced he was retiring as F1's medical delegate to become President of the FIA Institute for Motorsport Safety.

FIA president Max Mosley paid tribute to Watkins. 'Professor Watkins has made a unique contribution to improving the standards of safety and medical intervention in Formula One and indeed internationally throughout motorsport,' he said.

JANUARY 21

After sweeping the board with the revolutionary ground-effect car in 1978, most of the paddock assumed the Lotus cars would again be on top at the opening round of the 1979 season, the Argentine Grand Prix, held on this day. As it turned out the Ligier team had adapted best to the new ground-effect era and Jacques Laffite and Patrick Depailler took pole and second on the grid respectively. Laffite took the victory while local hero Carlos Reutemann had to settle for second in his Lotus.

The race also saw the debut of a young Italian driver named Elio de Angelis for the Shadow team. A popular paddock presence and a concert-standard pianist, de Angelis won the last race for Lotus in 1982 before team boss Colin Chapman died. De Angelis himself was killed while testing a Brabham at Paul Ricard in 1986.

JANUARY 22

Fangio continued his dominance in his home Grand Prix today in 1956 but he needed his teammate's help to do it. After mechanical problems with his Lancia-Ferrari had forced him to retire on lap 23, the team ordered his teammate Luigi Musso to pit and give his car to Fangio. Many of the other leaders had their own mechanical problems allowing Fangio, in Musso's car, to take the victory by half a minute.

Mike Hawthorne finished third in that race and in 1958 he became Britain's first ever World Champion, beating his great rival Stirling Moss. He retired immediately after winning the title but just three months later, on this day in 1959, he was killed in a car accident near Guildford. He was driving a Jaguar when it hit the kerb and crashed into a tree. The cause of the accident has never been conclusively explained.

JANUARY 23

The first F1 racer to emerge from Argentina since Fangio was Carlos Reutemann and he made his debut in stunning style at his home Grand Prix, today in 1972. He shocked most of the paddock with a brilliant qualifying effort which gave him pole position on his debut – something only ever previously achieved by Mario Andretti and since by Jacques Villeneuve. Normal service was resumed in the race when reigning World Champion Jackie Stewart took victory and Reutemann had to settle for seventh.

Five years later to the day and Reutemann had another British rival to deal with in the shape of James Hunt, who beat the Argentine to pole for the Brazilian Grand Prix at Interlagos. Reutemann was second on the grid but this time he had the last laugh when Hunt had handling problems late on and Carlos was able to pass him and take the victory.

JANUARY 24

Having let Alex Zanardi go after a disappointing 1999 season Williams were looking for someone to partner Ralf Schumacher for 2000. They settled on either Brazilian Bruno Junqueira or virtual unknown Jenson Button, who had recently picked up the prestigious McLaren Autosport BRDC Young Driver Award. The team arranged a 'shootout' test for them to fight for the drive, with Button coming out on top. Today in 2000 he was announced as F1's newest star and the British press went berserk at the rapid rise of the youngster who, only two years previously had been racing karts. Williams technical director Patrick Head said: 'He is remarkably mature for a 19-year-old and is definitely a star of the future.'

Today in 2005 one of the most colourful characters of F1 bowed out when Eddie Jordan announced he had sold his eponymous team to the Midland group from Russia. Although the team retained the Jordan name for one final season it was really the end for the team which always claimed to put the fun back into F1.

JANUARY 25

Niki Lauda was the reigning World Champion when the drivers lined up for the first race of the 1976 season in Brazil on this day. The race was the first to be started by a system of lights rather than the traditional flag but it didn't stop Lauda taking the victory. It was the start of a great run which saw him take four wins from the first six races. He looked odds-on to retain his championship until his horrific crash at the Nurburgring in August where he very nearly died.

Years later Lauda would become team principal of the Jaguar F1 team which was launched on this day in 2000. It was a rebranding of the Stewart team founded and run by Sir Jackie Stewart which Ford had bought. The new British racing green car was unveiled by drivers Eddie Irvine and Johnny Herbert but Sir Jackie announced he would be stepping down as team boss at the launch ceremony.

JANUARY 26

Carlos Pace was a talented Brazilian driver who was tragically killed in a plane crash in 1977. Today in 1975 he took his only F1 victory in his home race, the Brazilian Grand Prix at Interlagos. Pace delighted the home crowd by leading home a Brazilian 1-2 as Emerson Fittipaldi came in second. After Pace's death the Interlagos circuit was renamed the Autodromo Jose Carlos Pace in his honour.

The race was also significant for another driver who was tragically killed in a plane crash. Double World Champion Graham Hill started his own team in 1975 but he was still racing himself at the beginning of the season. The Brazilian GP was the last race he finished before he finally retired after 176 starts. He came home 12th, a lap down on the leaders.

JANUARY 27

The 1974 season had started well for McLaren with victory for Denny Hulme in the Argentine GP. The team's good form continued on this day at the Brazilian Grand Prix when Emerson Fittipaldi won his home race for the second year in succession. He had had to fight for it though as Ronnie Peterson in his Lotus had battled hard with Fittipaldi until a puncture forced him to concede the race.

In 11 years in Formula One Frenchman Rene Arnoux took seven victories. The first came today in 1980 at the Brazilian Grand Prix at Interlagos, the season curtain-raiser. His teammate Jean-Pierre Jabouille in the other Renault had taken pole position while Arnoux was forced to fight his way to victory from sixth on the grid.

JANUARY 28

When Brazilian Emerson Fittipaldi won the drivers' title in 1972 aged 25, he was the youngest ever champion (a record since surpassed by Fernando Alonso and Lewis Hamilton) and at the first race of the 1973 season, held today in Argentina, it looked like he would continue his domination when he took victory for Team Lotus. His rival Jackie Stewart finished third that day but would go on to take the title at the end of the season.

Today in 2002 marked the end of the road for Prost Grand Prix, the racing team run by the great French driver Alain Prost. With the loss of his major sponsors and Peugeot engines The Professor was not able to find any investors willing to save the team and it was put into liquidation. 'I received so many blows for months and years that it's almost a relief for me. I was lynched in the last couple of weeks and I see it as a total failure for France,' Prost said.

JANUARY 29

Despite the fact the Interlagos circuit has produced some exciting races over the years, the facilities are not great and it is not a favourite of the F1 circus. For the 1978 grand prix, held on this day, the race was moved to the Jacarepaguá circuit in the more glamorous setting of Rio de Janeirio. It made little difference to the outcome – Argentine Carlos Reutemann took victory for Ferrari, just as he had done at Interlagos the year before.

Reutemann's victory was also the first win in Formula One for the French tyre manufacturer Michelin who had entered the sport the previous year.

JANUARY 30

Every F1 fan's favourite minnow team was saved today in 2001 when Australian businessman Paul Stoddart purchased the Minardi team. Stoddard had been keen on entering the sport for some time and had bought up much of the old stock when the Tyrrell team was closed down. With the first race of the season in Australia little over a month away the team faced a mammoth task to make it onto the grid in time. 'It is undoubtedly a huge challenge but everyone is up for it,' said Stoddart.

Today in 2009 the McLaren team was mourning the loss of one of the most important figures in its history. Teddy Mayer, who helped Bruce McLaren found the team in 1963, passed away aged 73. Ron Dennis paid tribute to his predecessor. 'Teddy was one of motor racing's few truly great men. Bruce died tragically young in 1970, having won grands prix but no World Championships with his fledgling team,' he said, 'but when I bought into the team in 1980 Teddy had built on the foundations laid by Bruce, Tyler Alexander and himself and had already achieved a lot – two Formula One World Championships, as well as huge success in the States. I would like to pay tribute to Teddy's enormously valuable contribution, and to his immortal legacy.'

JANUARY 31

Today in 1997 the Williams-Renault FW19 was launched at the team factory in Oxfordshire. The car was the last in a series that had been highly successful for the team, as it would be the last to use Renault engines as the French manufacturer pulled out of the sport at the end of the season. It was also the last Williams designed by Adrian Newey who left the team to join McLaren. It was once again the class of the field though and won both the drivers' and constructers' titles, and remains the last championship-winning car Williams has produced.

After the phenomenal success Italian racer Valentino Rossi had on two wheels in MotoGP, speculation was rife that he was keen on a switch to Formula One. Today in 2006 he had his first public test in an F1 racer when he got behind the wheel of a Ferrari F2004 at Valencia. Halfway round his first lap he spun and ended up in the gravel trap. He did make a better impression on the second day but has yet to switch sports.

FORMULA ONE
On This Day

FEBRUARY

FEBRUARY 1

For the team that saw undoubtedly the most politicking in the F1 pitlane, British American Racing made an apt move today in 2001 when they appointed a well-known Conservative politician as non-executive chairman. Ken Clarke, a former Chancellor of the Exchequer and a member of the British Racing Drivers Club, took on the role but was unable to influence an upturn in fortunes for the team.

For a country with such a vast population India had never made an impact on F1 until today in 2005 when Narain Kathikeyan signed a contract with the Jordan team to become the first ever Indian driver in the top level of motorsport. Dubbed 'the fastest Indian in the world' he said: 'I've got the hopes of a nation behind me so I've no choice but to succeed now.' His best finish was fourth in the farcical US GP when only six cars took part, before he was dropped at the end of the season.

FEBRUARY 2

One of the consequences of Lewis Hamilton's immediate pace in his debut season with McLaren was the pressure he heaped upon his teammate, double World Champion Fernando Alonso. The Spaniard had thought he was to be Number 1 in the team and did not appreciate being challenged by the rookie. Alonso's Spanish fans inevitably took a dislike to Hamilton, although some of them took it far beyond friendly rivalry. Today in 2008 Hamilton was testing at Barcelona when he was confronted by a number of fans waving racist banners. BBC commentator David Croft explained: '(Some) were chanting nasty stuff and booing him when he made his way from the garage to the McLaren area at the back. We've never seen that at Formula One events.' Hamilton said: 'The truth is I feel somewhat sad. I love this country, especially the city of Barcelona. The people in Spain have always been very warm.'

FEBRUARY 3

Today in 2000 Daimler, the parent company of Mercedes, took up their option to buy a 40 per cent stake in the McLaren team, with whom they had enjoyed a successful partnership since 1995. The deal was also part of a plan for the two companies to produce sports cars.

In the wake of the global financial crisis and Honda pulling out of the sport there were rumours in the press in early 2009 that senior Daimler executives were questioning the company's F1 involvement, and that a decision to continue had only been passed by a narrow 3-2 vote of the board. Today in 2009 a Daimler spokesman denied the story and reaffirmed the company's commitment to the sport. 'There was no voting by the Daimler board of management concerning Formula One,' the spokesman told *autosport.com*. 'It is correct to say that we continue our commitment.'

FEBRUARY 4

Ligier proved their pace in the first race of the 1979 season was no fluke when Jacques Laffite took victory again at the Brazilian Grand Prix on this day to add to his win in Argentina two weeks earlier. His teammate Patrick Depailler came in second to cap a dominant weekend for the French team, but it would prove to be something of a false dawn as Laffite won no more races that season, and Ligier took just one more win with Depailler in Spain while Jody Scheckter and Ferrari wrapped up both championships.

Formula One cars are designed to be driven on race tracks but today in 2007 Nick Heidfeld found himself taking his BMW Sauber car for a spin on a frozen lake in St Moritz, Switzerland as part of an event for sponsors Credit Suisse. Heidfeld ran with special spiked tyres and the car's engine had to be warmed up every half hour to prevent it from freezing. 'That was quite a unique experience,' he said.

FEBRUARY 5

Manfred von Brauchitsch, the last surviving member of the Silver Arrows drivers, the elite band of racers who drove the legendary Mercedes-Benz grand prix cars between the wars, died on this day in 2003 aged 97. When Mercedes decided to start a factory racing team, team boss Alfred Neubauer hired von Brauchitsch to drive. The team's first race was the Eifelrennen at the Nurburgring in 1934 but to their dismay the new car was just over the 750kg weight limit. According to Neubauer, he and von Brauchitsch hit on the idea of scraping the white paint off the cars. The Silver Arrow was born and von Brauchitsch drove the car to victory in its first race.

He won two more races, the 1937 Monaco Grand Prix and the 1938 French Grand Prix but he was often cursed with bad luck and lost a number of races that were within his grasp, notably the 1935 German Grand Prix when he blew a tyre on the last lap, handing a famous victory to Tazio Nuvolari in an Alfa Romeo.

FEBRUARY 6

Niki Lauda was always regarded as one of the most canny and intelligent drivers on the grid and when he hung up his driving gloves after winning three world titles he turned his hand to business, running his own airline, and worked as a consultant to Ferrari. Today in 2001 he was appointed CEO of Ford's Premier Performance Division which effectively made him boss of the Jaguar F1 team. Sadly 'The Rat' was unable to lead the team to success and was fired in 2003.

Minardi has always been something of a proving ground for new talent in Formula One and today in 2001 another star of the future was confirmed as a driver with the Italian squad. Fernando Alonso, protégé of Flavio Briatore, spent one season with Minardi before graduating to the Renault team where he won back-to-back world titles.

FEBRUARY 7

Bruce McLaren's first F1 win came at the 1959 United States Grand Prix in December – the last race of that season. He followed that up by winning the next race, the season opening Argentine GP held today in 1960. It was a somewhat fortunate victory after Innes Ireland (Lotus) and Jo Bonnier (BRM) were both running ahead of him until mechanical failure ruined their races.

Today in 1981 the non-championship event the South African Grand Prix was held at Kyalami. A direct product of the FISA/FOCA war between the governing body and the independent teams that was raging in the early 1980s, only the independent FOCA teams took part. Carlos Reutemann took victory for Williams.

FEBRUARY 8

Hans Stuck Snr was a pre-war racing driver who lived an extraordinary life. After serving in the German army in the First World War, he became a dairy farmer and bought a car so he could transport his milk to market. Soon he was racing in and winning hill climb events and gained notoriety when he claimed he would win a race driving backwards. He reversed the gearbox on his car and did it. In 1926 he had a bet with an Austrian Count named Szichy about whose car was faster. Stuck won the bet and took the prize – the Count's wife Xenia.

An acquaintance of Hitler, he introduced the Nazi leader to Ferdinand Porsche which resulted in the creation of the legendary Auto Union team. He won three races in 1934 with the team but in 1937 he was sacked in acrimonious circumstances: the team said it was because he was too old but Stuck claimed it was because he had told his teammate how much he was earning. Stuck continued racing in hill climb events until he was 60 but he passed away on this day in 1978, aged 77. His son, Hans Stuck Jnr, went on to become an F1 driver in the 1970s.

FEBRUARY 9

On this day in 1909 the Indianapolis Motor Speedway Corporation was founded with former racing driver and entrepreneur Carl G Fisher as its first president. The first race was held later that year in August but it was a disaster. In the rush to open the new circuit Fisher and his partners had laid a track surface of crushed stone and tar but it quickly became apparent that it was sub-standard and it caused many accidents, with five people killed. In these appalling circumstances the 300-mile race was halted after 235 miles.

Rather than give up, Fisher had the track paved with more than three million bricks and the famous Brickyard circuit, the most famous motor racing track in America, was born. The first Indy 500 race was held in 1911 when Ray Harroun took victory. It is now the largest single-day sporting event in the world with 400,000 fans turning out every year.

FEBRUARY 10

By 1992 Ayrton Senna was unhappy at McLaren. Williams had become the major force in F1, and he was desperate to drive for them, even reportedly offering to drive for the team for nothing – but Williams had Prost lined up for 1993, and he vetoed Senna as a teammate. Undecided on what to do for the coming season, Senna had even secretly tested a Penske CART car with a view to moving to the American series. On this day in 1993 Ron Dennis appeared to make up his mind for him when he announced Michael Andretti and Mika Hakkinen as McLaren's drivers for the season, leaving Senna without a seat. Eventually the Brazilian backed down and did race for McLaren. He finally got the Williams drive the following year.

FEBRUARY 11

The first ever Brazilian Grand Prix was held in 1972 but it was a non-championship event, won by Carlos Reutemann. The first championship race was held today in 1973 at Interlagos – the event was bound to be popular as Emerson Fittipaldi was reigning World Champion, having become the first Brazilian to win the title in 1972. He did not disappoint the massive crowd that turned up to support him when he took victory in his Lotus ahead of Jackie Stewart and Denny Hulme.

There were three other Brazilians in the race that day but none had good fortune in their home event. Emerson's brother Wilson Fittipaldi retired on lap five when his Brabham overheated, Carlos Pace made it to lap nine before suspension failure on his Surtees-Ford put him out, while Luiz Bueno was not so bueno in his one and only World Championship race: he qualified last and then finished last.

FEBRUARY 12

Many sports stars will put their name to anything if it will earn them some more cash, but in 2001 Michael Schumacher was honoured by his hometown when he had a street named after him. The road in Kerpen that leads to his family's karting track was renamed at a special ceremony on this day. 'It's always comforting to see how much support I get every time I come home,' he said. 'It will be a great feeling to drive down that street.'

Before the corporation won back the TV rights to F1, the BBC had to make do with radio coverage. Today in 2001 the Beeb won an extension to the F1 radio contract. Bernie Ecclestone said: 'The massive radio following for Formula One has been very well served by BBC Radio 5 Live in the UK. When something works that well, it's best left in place.'

FEBRUARY 13

Yet another grand old name was leaving the sport today in 1997 when Alain Prost bought the Ligier team and renamed it after himself. The team was started by former French rugby international Guy Ligier in the late sixties and had some success in the seventies and eighties but by 1992 Ligier himself had left. The team passed into the hands of Flavio Briatore but Prost's acquisition of the team was seen as a fresh start for the all-French squad. That first year, 1997, would turn out to be Les Bleus best season and the team went bust in 2001.

Another famous French racing name also bowed out on this day, when Maurice Trintignant died in 2005, aged 87. He was robbed of his prime driving years by the Second World War but he still managed to win the Monaco GP twice and was the last man to drive a Bugatti in a grand prix.

FEBRUARY 14

The most expensive and ostentatious F1 car launch took place today in 1997 when McLaren unveiled their new challenger, the MP4/12 at Alexandra Palace in London complete with the Spice Girls and Jamiroquai. Title sponsor Marlboro had left for Ferrari so the new car featured a brand new livery which was partly silver in homage to the traditional racing colours of Mercedes-Benz. It performed quite well on the track as David Coulthard took two wins and Mika Hakkinen one as the team geared up for 1998 when they dominated the championship.

One of the honoured guests at the launch was 92-year-old Manfred von Brauchitsch who was the first man to win a grand prix in a Silver Arrow Mercedes at the Eifelrennen on the old Nurburgring in June 1934 – the first race Mercedes ran in silver livery. Von Brauchitsch was the last surviving member of the pre-war Silver Arrows.

FEBRUARY 15

Former Formula One driver Aguri Suzuki realised his dream of an all-Japanese F1 team today in 2006 when he announced Takuma Sato and Yuji Ide were to be the drivers for his new Honda backed team, Super Aguri. Sato had raced in F1 previously with Jordan and BAR and acquitted himself well with the small team, but Ide was inexperienced and struggled badly. He only managed four races before the FIA withdrew his super licence forcing the team to replace him with Franck Montagny.

The threat of a manufacturer-led breakaway series lessened further today in 2007 when Renault formally left the Grand Prix Manufacturers' Association (GPMA) following meetings between the body and the FIA which sought to clarify the future of F1. The French company followed Toyota in leaving the GPMA, leaving only BMW, Daimler and Honda in the organisation.

FEBRUARY 16

Jean Behra, a French racing driver from the 1950s, was born on this day in 1921 in Nice. Although undoubtedly a fast driver, Behra failed to win any F1 World Championship races, although he did win non-championship races at Pau, Bordeaux, Bari and Morocco. He was teammate to both Stirling Moss and Juan Manuel Fangio at Maserati, and later drove for BRM.

In 1959 he signed for Ferrari to partner Tony Brooks but he didn't last long with the Italian team. After retiring from the French Grand Prix at Reims he fell out with team manager Romolo Tavoni and punched him. He was sacked immediately and less than a month later he was killed in a sports car race when he crashed his Porsche and was thrown from the car and hit a flagpole.

FEBRUARY 17

Back in 2000 Jenson Button was the young British driver making the headlines when he bagged a full race seat at Williams, aged just 20. At the time Lewis Hamilton was just a 15-year-old school boy but he was already a big name in karting circles and had been signed up by the McLaren-Mercedes Driver Support Programme after he famously approached Ron Dennis and asked to one day drive for his team when he was just ten-years-old.

Today in 2000 young Lewis told the *London Evening Standard* he too wanted to make it to F1. 'If you are good enough you are old enough – I want to just make sure that it's the right time when I move up', he said. 'But I would like to beat Jenson and become the youngest-ever F1 driver.' Lewis was 23 when he graduated to F1, but he did beat Jenson to becoming World Champion.

FEBRUARY 18

The American Nascar series was in mourning today in 2001 when Dale Earnhardt was killed after an accident in the Daytona 500 in Florida. Earnhardt, 49, was a seven-time Nascar Winston Cup champion and was considered the Ayrton Senna of his sport – a brilliant and aggressive driver who everyone thought was invincible. Nascar chairman Bill France Jr said: 'Nascar has lost its greatest driver ever.'

Monaco is well used to the sound of Formula One cars roaring around the tiny principality, but not usually in February. Today in 2007 the Ferrari team turned up three months earlier than the usual May slot for the grand prix to film an advertisement for fuel partners Shell. Irish drivers Michael Cullen and Paddy Shovlin drove an F2003 around the streets which would form part of a huge advert featuring the Ferraris driving through famous cities including New York, Sydney, Hong Kong and Rome.

FEBRUARY 19

With his dyed hair and loose driving overalls, Jacques Villeneuve has always been a bit rock'n'roll and today in 2007 he proved it when he released his debut album Private Paradise. Jacques wrote six of the 13 songs himself and sang lead vocals on them all. 'I bought a guitar in '96 when I started racing in Formula One, and started writing some songs,' he said, adding: 'I am stupidly passionate about music, it has become a bit of a drug.'

Until Fernando Alonso came along Spain really had very little heritage when it came to Formula One drivers – Alonso was the first Spaniard ever to win a grand prix. Today in 1996 Antonio Creus, one of the unsuccessful Spanish F1 drivers, died aged 71. He started only one race, the 1960 Argentine GP but failed to finish.

FEBRUARY 20

The Simtek team will always be remembered for the fact that Roland Ratzenberger died in one of their cars on the same weekend as Senna was killed, but in their short history the team did show promise at times, especially considering they operated with an unbelievably tiny staff of just 35 people – top teams today employ nearer 1,000. Today in 1995 Dutchman Jos Verstappen signed to race with the team for the 1995 season. Loss of sponsorship money meant it would be Simtek's last in F1.

The post-script to the terrible accident that killed Ayrton Senna was a drawn out trial that hung over the heads of the Williams team and designer Adrian Newey for years. Today in 1997, three years after the crash, the trial which would rule on the cause of the accident began in Imola, just a stone's throw from the circuit where Senna was killed. Frank Williams, Patrick Head and Newey were all charged with 'culpable homicide' along with three other race officials from the Imola circuit. After a trial lasting nearly a year all six were cleared of all charges.

FEBRUARY 21

English racing driver Peter Gethin was born on this day in 1940. He drove 30 races in F1, mainly for McLaren and BRM, and took just one win: the 1971 Italian Grand Prix at Monza when he went from fourth to first place on the very last lap to win the closest ever finish in F1 history; he was just 0.01 seconds ahead of Ronnie Peterson. Gethin's average speed was 150.75mph making it the fastest ever race in the history of the F1 World Championship. The record stood until the 2003 Italian GP when Michael Schumacher broke it with an average speed of 153.84mph.

Four years later on the same day Ferenc Szisz passed away aged 60. The Hungarian driver was the winner of the first ever race to use the title 'Grand Prix', the French Grand Prix at Le Mans in 1906. After he passed away, another man, rumoured to be his brother, impersonated Szisz in Hungary until he too died in 1970.

FEBRUARY 22

The Daytona 500, the most important race in the NASCAR calendar, was first held on this day in 1959. Known as the 'Super Bowl of stock car racing', the first race was won by Lee Petty in unusual circumstances. Petty and Johnny Beauchamp were lapping a backmarker when they crossed the finish line. Beauchamp was initially declared the winner but after three days of reviewing photos and film of the finish, the race officials reversed their decision and gave the win to Petty.

Triple World Champion Niki Lauda was born on this day in 1949 in Vienna. The Austrian driver initially borrowed a large amount of money to buy his way into F1 but then went on to win the World Championship twice with Ferrari and then again with McLaren after two years out of the sport.

FEBRUARY 23

One of the more bizarre incidents in the history of motor racing happened today in 1958 in Cuba when Juan Manuel Fangio was kidnapped by Cuban rebel supporters of Fidel Castro and Che Guevara. Fangio had won the Havana GP the previous year but the rebels kidnapped him at gunpoint in his hotel before the race. The Argentine driver was remarkably calm about the whole affair and was released after the race was over. He was sympathetic to his captors and their political aims and even refused to identify them afterwards. Years later he returned to Cuba as a guest of state and said: 'Two big dreams have come true for me: returning to Cuba and meeting Fidel Castro.'

The race went ahead without him but ended in disaster when local driver Armando Garcia Cifuentes crashed his Ferrari into the crowd, killing six and injuring 30 of the estimated 200,000 spectators.

FEBRUARY 24

The official report into the accident which killed Ayrton Senna was made public today in 1995. The investigation was carried out by Italian magistrate Maurizio Passarini and ran to more than 500 pages. The inquiry drew evidence from a host of experts and concluded the crash was probably caused by a steering failure on Senna's Williams car. This was far from the end of the story however as the trial would rumble on for years.

Formula One fans were celebrating today in 2009 when the BBC announced it would be bringing back Fleetwood Mac's The Chain as the title music for F1 coverage. The iconic tune was the theme for the BBC's *Grand Prix* programme from 1978 until 1997 when coverage switched to ITV. On hearing that the music was to return Murray Walker said: 'Every time I hear that music, I get butterflies, because I know that when it stops, I start.'

FEBRUARY 25

The most famous and successful engine in Formula One history is the Cosworth DFV which won on its grand prix debut in a Lotus with Jim Clark at the wheel and eventually took a staggering 155 wins before it was retired. On this day in 2004 Cosworth announced it was to start making the legendary power unit again, as demand for parts was still high thanks to classic racing series which still used it.

The 500-year-old cobbles of Moscow's Red Square were brought straight into contact with the most modern motoring technology today in 2005 when the Jordan team chose the spot to host their latest car launch. The team had recently been bought by the Russian-backed Midland group. 'We want our F1 team to have a Russian flavour so it was very important to introduce ourselves appropriately to the media and business here in Moscow,' explained Jordan's then managing director Colin Kolles.

FEBRUARY 26

Honda Racing surprised the F1 world today in 2007 when it unveiled its Green Earth livery which saw the cars simply carry a map of the world and no sponsorship logos. Instead sponsors were urged to make a donation to an environmental charity and get a mention on Honda's website. 'We hope that in raising awareness and highlighting the issues we will encourage members of the public to come together and help take on the challenge of climate change,' said the team's chief executive Nick Fry. The more cynical critics wondered if the team's failure to land a title sponsor for the season had influenced the decision to go for the radical scheme.

Although Honda were trumpeting their new-found environmental concern as ground-breaking, *Autosport* magazine revealed Formula One had actually been carbon neutral since 1997. The FIA had been financially supporting the Scolel Te project in southern Mexico which offset all carbon emissions from F1 and the World Rally Championship.

FEBRUARY 27

One of the most extraordinary motor races ever took place today in 1927 in Paris when a group of drivers competed in a hill climb event *inside* a six-storey building. The race was a promotional event for the Garage Banville, a new luxury garage and sports club for rich Parisians. Organised by Robert Benoist, a famous racing driver of the day, a selection of 15 racers drove round a course that used the ramps inside the building and even a section of the roof. There was no winner as it had been decided not to time the laps lest the driver's competitive instincts should cause an accident but it was a big success nonetheless and made the garage famous.

Nearly 80 years later and motor racing stunts were still being used to get the public interested. On this day in 2005 Australian driver Mark Webber drove his Williams BMW F1 car across the world-famous Sydney Harbour Bridge, in the build up to the Australian Grand Prix in Melbourne. After driving 12 times across the 503 metre-long bridge Webber said: 'Thundering with 900 bhp over that time-honoured structure was an amazing feeling. The engine sound over the ocean was fantastic.'

FEBRUARY 28

Legendary American racing driver Mario Andretti was born on this day in 1940. He is the last American driver to have an impact in Formula One and won the World Championship in 1978 with Lotus. He is the only driver to have won the Indianapolis 500 (1969), the Daytona 500 (1967), and the F1 World Championship. His son Michael drove for McLaren in 1993 with little success.

Andretti shares his birthday with French driver Sebastien Bourdais, who was born today in 1979 in Le Mans. Like Andretti, Bourdais raced with great success in America, winning four Champ Car titles in a row. He switched to F1 in 2008.

FEBRUARY 29

Frank Williams famously missed out on the chance to sign Ayrton Senna when the Brazilian was a young unknown and it emerged today in 2008 that Williams also had the chance to sign Lewis Hamilton when he was still racing in Formula Three Euroseries.

Williams co-owner Patrick Head told *Autosport* Hamilton and his father had got in touch in 2004. 'They rang up and said "can we come and see you?" And they came in and said "Ron Dennis has dropped us". We were with BMW at the time and I think Frank rang (BMW's then-motorsport director) Mario Theissen and said "look, this guy looks as if he could be pretty good and whatever and he has come to us saying can we help him." And I think Mario said they weren't prepared to provide any support and we weren't in a position financially where we could finance his racing. So much to Frank's annoyance, he could have had Lewis in a Williams.'

FORMULA ONE
On This Day

MARCH

MARCH 1

Two British World Champions got their seasons off to the best possible starts on this day. First, Jackie Stewart in 1969 who took victory in the South African Grand Prix at Kyalami. He took the lead at the end of the first lap from Jack Brabham and stayed there until the chequered flag to win the first race of the season in which he would claim the first of his three drivers' titles.

Also on this day in 1992 Nigel Mansell laid down a marker to the rest of the paddock with his dominant performance in the South African Grand Prix at Kyalami. No one had come near him in qualifying and in the race he sprinted away to win from Riccardo Patrese, his teammate in the other Williams-Renault. It was a snapshot of how the rest of the season would play out with Mansell finally winning the World Championship after coming so close three times before.

MARCH 2

The Ligier team was causing controversy today in 1995 with the launch of their new car. Rival teams claimed the car was simply a Benetton with a different livery which would have made sense as Flavio Briatore and Tom Walkinshaw controlled both teams. The other teams were unhappy because it meant Ligier had seemingly had to bear none of the costs of designing and building their own car.

Two new teams did their first competitive running today in 2002 in qualifying for the first race of the season in Australia. Toyota made their long-awaited debut with Mika Salo and Allan McNish driving, while French manufacturer Renault was back as a constructor in F1 for the first time since 1985, having taken over the Benetton team, with Jarno Trulli and Jenson Button piloting the cars.

MARCH 3

Mike 'the Bike' Hailwood was already one of the world's top motorbike riders when he switched to four wheels to try his hand at grand prix racing. He was on the grid for the South African Grand Prix at Kyalami today in 1973 when his car was hit by Clay Regazzoni's BRM which then burst into flames with Regazzoni unconscious at the wheel. Hailwood immediately dived into the flames, undid Regazzoni's seatbelts and dragged him clear of the burning wreckage. Clay was taken to hospital with minor burns while Hailwood was awarded the George Medal for his bravery.

The 2002 season kicked off on this day with the first race in Melbourne, Australia. Michael Schumacher won in his Ferrari but the real hero was Mark Webber, the Australian driver making his Formula One debut for the Minardi team which was then owned by Australian Paul Stoddart. Webber finished fifth for the minnows earning him two points and a fantastic reaction from his boss and home crowd.

MARCH 4

A classic race took place at Kyalami today in 1978 when Mario Andretti, Riccardo Patrese and Patrick Depailler looked set to battle it out for victory. No one gave much thought to the Swiss driver Ronnie Peterson who started well down the grid in his Lotus, but Patrese's engine let go with just 15 laps left, and then Andretti ran out of fuel. Peterson was able to catch Depailler and the two raced the last lap side by side, banging wheels twice as neither wanted to relent. On the penultimate corner Peterson got the upper hand and won the race by just three car lengths.

The racing took a back seat at the Australian Grand Prix on this day in 2001 when a marshal named Graham Beveridge was killed by a bouncing wheel from Jacques Villeneuve's BAR car after he had collided with Ralf Schumacher's Williams-BMW. The two drivers were unhurt.

MARCH 5

One of the most bizarre accidents occurred in the South African Grand Prix at Kyalami on this day in 1977. Renzo Zorzi was forced to pull over on lap 21 after his Shadow car developed a fuel pipe problem. A small fire started and two marshals crossed the track on the blind side of a brow of a hill with fire extinguishers to put it out. At that moment Welshman Tom Pryce and German Hans Struck came over the hill racing side by side. Pryce hit one of the marshals named Jansen van Vuuren, killing him instantly, while the fire extinguisher he was carrying hit Pryce on the head and killed him as well. His car carried on down the main straight and hit Jacques Laffite's Ligier at the first corner, although the Frenchman was not hurt.

As always in motorsport, the race continued and up at the front Niki Lauda won on his way to his second World Championship title.

MARCH 6

Mario Andretti is one of only a handful of American drivers to make his mark in F1 and today in 1971 he took his first ever victory when he won the South African GP at Kyalami for Ferrari. He went on to become World Champion in 1978.

Minardi were keen to sign Brit Justin Wilson for the 2003 season and even designed a bigger car to take his 6ft 4in frame, but to secure the drive he needed to raise £2m in sponsorship money. He and his manager, ex-F1 racer Jonathan Palmer, came up with a unique way of raising the money. They launched Justin Wilson Plc on this day in 2003 and invited investors to buy shares in his future earnings. The scheme was a success and he had the money raised by June 2003.

MARCH 7

Another driver having trouble with his larger than average size was Nigel Mansell who had signed up for McLaren for the 1995 season to partner Mika Hakkinen. Our Nige turned up at the factory on this day to discover his rather portly frame would not fit into the McLaren cockpit. Hakkinen said: 'Driving it is like running the London Marathon in a pair of running shoes which are too small. I know he (Mansell) has problems and he has suffered from bruising to his hands and arms. If it is bad for me, it is much worse for him.' Nige had to sit out the first two races while a bigger cockpit was built.

Today in 1999 Eddie Irvine finally reached the top step of the podium when he won the Australian Grand Prix. It was the first race of the season and the McLarens of Hakkinen and Coulthard were dominant in qualifying but fragile in the race, both dropping out with mechanical problems to leave Eddie a clear path to victory with his teammate Michael Schumacher coming home eighth after problems at the start.

MARCH 8

After years of Williams' domination the F1 circus turned up at Melbourne for the opening round of the 1998 World Championship to find the team from Grove was no longer top dog. The McLaren-Mercedes cars locked out the front row with Mika Hakkinen just ahead of David Coulthard. The race, run on this day, was to prove controversial when Hakkinen came into the pits on lap 36 thinking he had been called in by the team. They waved him on but he had lost the lead to Coulthard, who moved over for his teammate just before the end to give the Finnish driver the win.

The team was heavily criticised and there was talk of a pre-race agreement by the two drivers but it was later revealed someone had hacked into Hakkinen's radio and told him to pit.

MARCH 9

For such a famous and successful team McLaren were having a lean time of it in the mid-1990s as Williams ruled the tracks. Today in 1997 the team showed the signs that they were finally on their way back to the top when David Coulthard won the first round of the championship in Australia. It was McLaren's first win in 50 races.

The race was also notable for being the first to be covered by ITV since it had won the rights to cover F1 from the BBC. Murray Walker was joined by the excellent Martin Brundle in the commentary box. The race also marked the first appearance on the F1 circuit of the Lola team. The famous marque had run successful cars in all sorts of formulae but found F1 a little tougher. The two drivers Vincenzo Sospiri and Ricardo Rosset failed to qualify.

MARCH 10

The opening race of the 1991 season took place on this day with the United States Grand Prix in Phoenix. Senna won in his McLaren-Honda from Prost in second in his Ferrari. There were some notable new faces at the race. Future World Champion Mika Hakkinen made his first grand prix start for Lotus, and impressed by qualifying in 13th. It was also the first Formula One race for the Jordan team.

The 1996 Australian Grand Prix was notable for the stunning debut performance of newcomer Jacques Villeneuve in the Williams car. The son of legendary driver Gilles Villeneuve, Jacques arrived as the Indycar champion and immediately outshone teammate Damon Hill to take pole. Hill beat him in the race but the talking point was Martin Brundle's spectacular crash in the Jordan at the first corner. He was flat out doing 290kph when he hit the back of Johnny Herbert and David Coulthard and was launched into the air, ripping his car in two. Remarkably he was not hurt and made the re-start in the spare car.

MARCH 11

The world loves an underdog and that is perhaps why Minardi was such a popular team over the years despite the fact it was historically one of the least successful outfits the sport has ever seen. Such a commitment to losing has allowed the team to build up a worldwide following – there is even a British based fan club named the West Lavington Association of Minardi Enthusiasts. The team never won a race or even achieved a podium and almost half of the 38 points the team won in its history were scored by Pierluigi Martini who started from second on the grid for the United States GP on this day in 1990. It was Minardi's only front row start in its entire history. He finished seventh.

Kimi Raikkonen proved he is just as fast on snow as on tarmac today in 2007 when he won the 24-kilometre Enduro Sprint event at the Kopparberg King race in Finland. He competed under the name 'James Hunt' – the racer to whom he is often compared.

MARCH 12

After a broken leg had put paid to Michael Schumacher's chances of the 1999 World Championship and Eddie Irvine hadn't quite been able to do the job in his absence, Schumacher was determined to get it right in 2000 and deliver Ferrari's first drivers' title since 1979. He must have been worried when he was beaten in qualifying for the Australian GP by both McLarens but in the race both Hakkinen and Coulthard suffered engine failures and Schumi took the win with his new teammate Rubens Barrichello second. He had started as he meant to go on and was World Champion by the end of the year.

Today in 2006 it was a similar story, this time at the Bahrain GP. Again Schumacher took the win in the opening round of the season and again he was followed dutifully home by his teammate, this time Felipe Massa.

MARCH 13

Brazilian racing fans were quite spoilt in the early days of the Brazilian Grand Prix when Emerson Fittipaldi and Carlos Pace won three out of the first four races held there. After 1975 they would have to wait another eight years for a Brazilian winner but it happened today in 1983 when Nelson Piquet won the race in Rio de Janeiro driving for Bernie Ecclestone's Brabham team.

There was drama during the race when reigning World Champion Keke Rosberg pitted for fuel and his Williams caught fire. He jumped out of the car while the crew put the fire out and then got back in the car and drove through the field to finish second. All his effort was for nothing in the end as he was disqualified for receiving a push in the pits.

MARCH 14

Until 1983 non-championship races were common throughout the Formula One season and today in 1964 one of these, The Daily Mirror Trophy event took place at Snetterton in West Sussex. The race was won by Innes Ireland, a one-time Lotus driver and winner of the 1961 USA Grand Prix, but the event was beset by terrible weather. Driving sleet and snow forced the organisers to cut the distance from 50 to 35 laps while many drivers, including Graham Hill, crashed out.

Today in 1993 Alain Prost showed that a year off had not dulled his skills as he took pole and then victory in his first race back in the sport for the Williams team at the South African GP at Kyalami. While it was an impressive feat to win after a year of no driving, Prost was undoubtedly helped by the fact his Williams-Renault car was the class of the field and he went on to take his fourth title virtually unchallenged that season as Senna toiled in an uncompetitive McLaren-Ford.

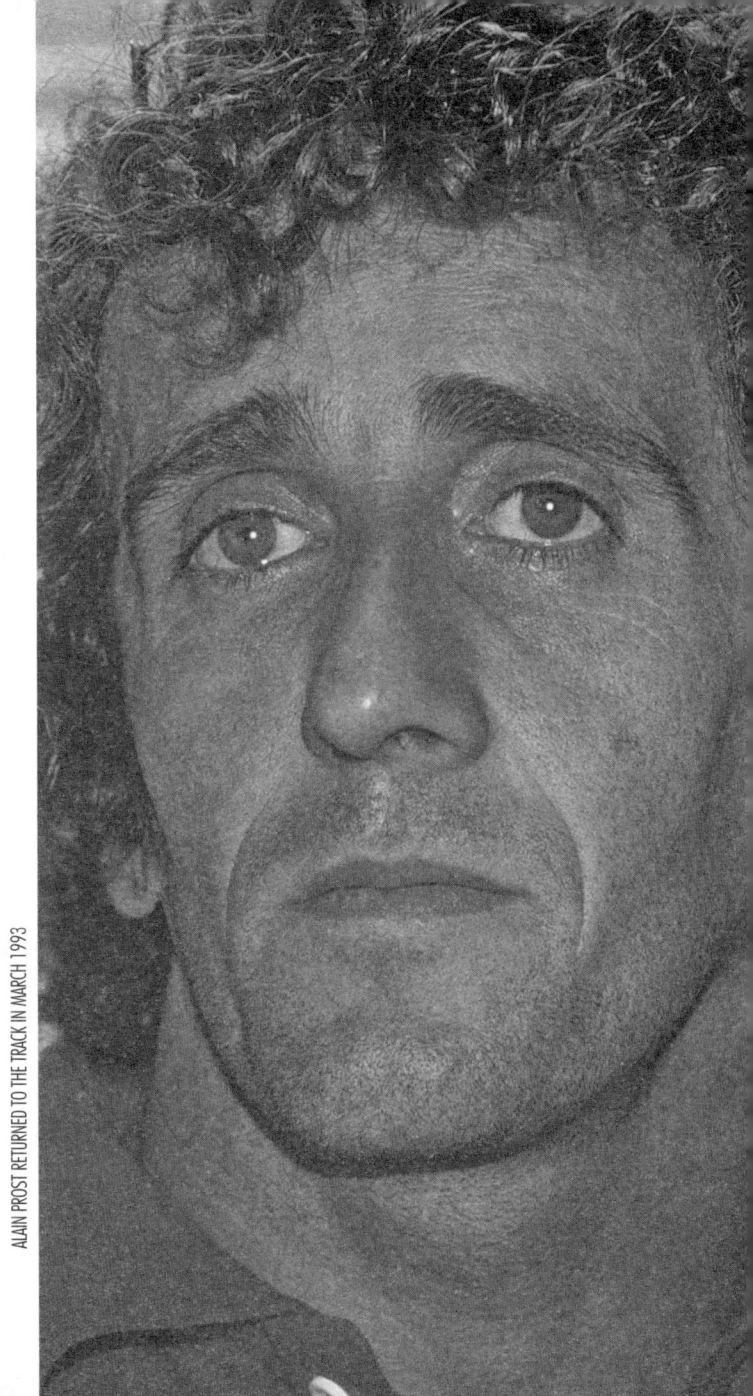

MARCH 15

After a winter of political wrangling between the teams' representative body FOCA and the governing body FISA, the F1 circus finally turned their attention to racing on this day in 1981 at the United States Grand Prix West at Long Beach, California. World Champion Alan Jones picked up where he had left off the previous season by leading home Carlos Reutemann in a Williams 1-2. The day before Riccardo Patrese made a little bit of history by claiming pole – his first and the only one the Arrows team would ever achieve in their 24-year history.

Meanwhile on the very same day, thousands of miles away at a very wet Brands Hatch track in England, a star in the making was continuing his rise to the top. Ayrton Senna, just 20 years old, lined up for just his second event in a racing car, a Formula Ford 1600 race. He displayed the wet-weather mastery that would become legendary by winning the race by nearly ten seconds from the second-placed man. He won £70 for his troubles.

MARCH 16

The Benetton team shot to prominence in the mid-nineties when the team powered Michael Schumacher to his first two drivers' titles. After he left for Ferrari in 1996 and took a glut of key technical people with him the team slipped back down the field. Today in 2000 carmaker Renault decided to return to the sport it had abandoned after 1997 and bought the team from the Benetton family. 'I said we would return one day to Formula One. It is the pinnacle of motorsport, a school of excellence for responsiveness, agility, technological skills,' said Renault chairman Louis Schweitzer. Five years later Fernando Alonso won the World Championship with the team.

After losing out on the 2007 championship at the last race of the season, Lewis Hamilton started 2008 in the best possible fashion by winning the opening round of the 2008 season at Melbourne, Australia on this day.

MARCH 17

After a good 2001 season for Williams when the team picked up four victories they were expected to push on in 2002 and challenge Ferrari for both championships. Today in 2002 Ralf Schumacher led home Juan Pablo Montoya for a Williams 1-2 at the Malaysian Grand Prix at Sepang. No one knew it at the time but the race was one of only two that Ferrari did not win all season in a truly dominant year for the Maranello squad. The other was a David Coulthard victory for McLaren at Monaco.

Further down the field Takuma Sato committed the cardinal sin for any racing driver by running into the back of his teammate Giancarlo Fisichella. The two Jordan cars had to pit and though both were eventually repaired and sent back out, any hope of a points finish was long gone.

MARCH 18

Not many drivers win on their debut for a new team, still less achieve the feat with the world's most famous squad, Ferrari. Finnish driver Kimi Raikkonen did just that on this day in 2007 at the Australian Grand Prix. He had defected from previous team McLaren after a number of race victories but no championships with the Woking wonders. McLaren had replaced him with young hotshot Lewis Hamilton who impressed everyone in the paddock and around the world with his measured and mature drive to third in his first ever Formula One race.

Brazilian driver Carlos Pace only ever won one grand prix, his home event at Interlagos in 1975 but today in 1977 he was killed in a light aircraft accident along with his friend and fellow racer Marivaldo Fernandes. The track at Interlagos was renamed the Autodromo Jose Carlos Pace in his honour after the crash.

MARCH 19

Fernando Alonso and Giancarlo Fisichella were teammates at Renault for both the 2005 and 2006 seasons. In those two years Alonso won two World Championships and 14 races. By contrast Fisichella, who had always been highly regarded in the paddock, won just two races. The first was the 2005 Australian Grand Prix, and the second came on this day in 2006 at the Malaysian Grand Prix. Fisi took pole and led from flag to flag after Alonso was accidentally over-fuelled which ruined his strategy. Just as in 2005 though, Fisichella could not build on his early season victory and it was Alonso that took the title again that season.

The race was also one of those rare occasions when Michael Schumacher was beaten by his teammate. In a day that was hardly stellar for either of the Ferraris Felipe Massa finished fifth ahead of Michael, sixth.

MARCH 20

Fernando Alonso took his first win of the season in the Malaysian Grand Prix at Sepang today in 2005 on his way to his first World Championship. Alonso led home Toyota's Jarno Trulli and Williams' Nick Heidfeld to end Ferrari's amazing run of 22 consecutive podium finishes which had begun at the 2003 Italian Grand Prix. After the race Alonso became the first Spaniard to lead the drivers' standings in the history of the sport.

Two other drivers in the field that day were Anthony Davidson who was making his only appearance for the Honda team and was deputising for the ill Takuma Sato, and Narain Karthikeyan who was making his F1 debut with Jordan and in doing so became the first ever Indian to race in the sport.

MARCH 21

As with any top international sport, politicking is never far from the F1 paddock and today in 1982 two drivers paid the price. The political battle for the control of the sport between the Fédération Internationale du Sport Automobile (FISA) and the Formula One Constructors Association (FOCA) started to boil over at the 1982 Brazilian GP. Brabham's Nelson Piquet and Williams' Keke Rosberg came first and second on the track, but were disqualified for having underweight cars. The two FOCA teams had used a loophole in the regulations to include water tanks which they claimed were for brake cooling but were in fact just ballast. FISA-aligned Renault protested and their driver Alain Prost was given the win.

By 2004 everyone was beginning to get a little bit sick of Ferrari and Michael Schumacher dominating F1 but on this day Schumi picked up his second victory of the season at the Malaysian GP. Although not quite a crushing performance the win for the Red Baron was one of 13 he would pick up that season on his way to yet another world title.

MARCH 22

Nigel Mansell took victory in the Mexican Grand Prix today in 1992 to make it two wins out of two for the mustachioed Englishman. As was the case for most of the season there was no one to touch Mansell in his Williams-Renault and he was followed home by his teammate Riccardo Patrese for another Williams 1-2 in the last Mexican Grand Prix to date.

A young Michael Schumacher provided the only slight challenge to the Williams in his Benetton-Ford when he finished third. It was his first ever podium finish in F1.

MARCH 23

More famous for his exploits on two wheels rather than four, Mike 'the Bike' Hailwood was the most loved motorcycle star of his era. He won ten World Championships in motorcycle racing and the European F2 Championship. He won the George Medal for his heroic rescue of Clay Regazzoni from his burning F1 car, but a big accident at the Nurburgring in a McLaren ended his own car racing days. In 1978 he made a surprise comeback to bikes after 11 years out and duly won the Isle of Man TT race on a Ducati. On this day in 1981 Mike was killed in a road accident near Birmingham.

The Malaysian GP held on this day in 2003 was another one for 'firsts', as Fernando Alonso started on pole for the first time and then finished third to become the first Spaniard to achieve a podium finish in F1. On the top step was Kimi Raikkonen who was celebrating his first ever win in the sport.

MARCH 24

Ayrton Senna won his home race, the Brazilian Grand Prix, for the first time on this day in 1991 at Interlagos. It was the first time the fanatical Brazilian crowd had seen a home winner since Nelson Piquet in 1986 but Senna had to work extremely hard for it. He held off challenges from both Nigel Mansell and Riccardo Patrese and survived gearbox problems which forced him to drive the last seven laps in sixth gear – nearly stalling on some of the slow corners. Then the heavens opened and Senna gestured to the marshals to stop the race, but it continued and he won by just 2.9 seconds from Patrese. Senna had taken a magnificent win but was so exhausted he had to be lifted out his car.

His McLaren teammate Gerhard Berger took third but was lucky to start let alone finish as his car caught fire on the grid but blew out allowing the Austrian to race on.

MARCH 25

Alain Prost has twice won the Brazilian Grand Prix on this day. The first was at Rio de Janeiro in 1984 when he took victory for McLaren from Keke Rosberg in the Williams and Elio de Angelis. Two notable debutantes that day were Martin Brundle who had been signed by Tyrrell, and a young Ayrton Senna who lined up for Toleman, making his F1 debut in his home race. An engine problem ruined his day, putting him out on lap eight.

Six years later to the day and Prost won again, this time at Interlagos. By now though Senna had taken Prost's place at McLaren and had already won his first drivers' title. He looked to be heading for his first win on home soil until he collided with backmarker Satoru Nakajima and had to pit. This handed victory to his old nemesis Prost – it was his 40th win and his first for Ferrari. Senna finished third behind his teammate Gerhard Berger.

MARCH 26

Nigel Mansell had the honour of being the last driver to be personally selected by Enzo Ferrari himself. He signed up for the 1989 season but winter testing showed the car's new electronic gearbox to be chronically unreliable. Mansell was so convinced the car would not last the distance at the first race in Brazil on this day that he booked a flight home that left halfway through the race. He surprised everyone, not least himself, by winning from sixth on the grid.

After just one dismal showing at the Australian GP where both cars failed to qualify and were some 11 seconds off the pace, today in 1997 the Lola team announced they were pulling out of Formula One. It was a sorry end for the team which had such a proud heritage of racing in other formulae and for supplying other F1 teams with chassis. The fallout from the F1 debacle led the company into administration shortly afterwards.

MARCH 27

Ulsterman John Watson had a reputation as something of a specialist in surging drives through the pack and today in 1983 he showed why when he took victory in the United States Grand Prix West at Long Beach, California. After starting 22nd on the grid Wattie scythed his way through the field to win the race for McLaren. It is the furthest back from which a modern F1 driver has won a race. To cap a remarkable race for McLaren Watson's teammate Niki Lauda followed him up the order finishing second after starting 23rd.

Ayrton Senna started his first grand prix in a Williams car today in 1994 at the Brazilian race at Interlagos but he was overshadowed by Michael Schumacher who took victory for Benetton. Senna spun while trying to catch him as Schumi announced himself as Senna's new rival-in-chief.

MARCH 28

It was a different story at Senna's home race the previous year when he came through to win an incident-packed Brazilian GP. Senna overcame rain, a safety car period and the performance disadvantage of his McLaren-Ford against the Williams-Renaults to take his second and last victory on home soil. It was also McLaren's 100th F1 victory.

It is well documented that Michael Schumacher is a big football fan and not a bad player either. Today in 2001 he got his shot at the big time when he played up front alongside Brazilian World Cup winner Ronaldo in a charity match watched by a crowd of 40,000 at the Maracana Stadium in Rio de Janeiro. Schumi was guilty of some dreadful finishing before he finally got on the score sheet with a second half penalty. 'It was great fun playing alongside Schumacher,' said Ronaldo. 'He by no means looked out of place. We even worked on some neat one-twos together.'

MARCH 29

Carlos Reutemann may have won the Brazilian GP today in 1981 but he lost at least one friend in teammate Alan Jones. Reutemann was leading the race in the closing stages with Jones just behind him. Jones, as the reigning World Champion and Williams team leader, expected Reutemann to let him through and the team held out pit boards telling him to move over lap after lap. Everyone assumed he would do it on the final lap but he didn't and took the chequered flag. Jones was furious and as the season wore on and Reutemann put together a decent tilt at the championship, he had to do it without Jones' help.

At the 1998 Australian GP the McLarens had pulverised the opposition with Hakkinen and Coulthard finishing a full lap ahead of anyone else. At the next race in Brazil on this day they proved Australia was no fluke by doing exactly the same thing with Hakkinen leading home another McLaren 1-2 as the Finnish driver began his title-winning season in style. Schumacher got a little closer but was still more than a minute behind the Woking cars at the end of the race.

MARCH 30

Carlos Reutemann won the South African GP today in 1974 and became the first Argentine winner in F1 since Juan Manuel Fangio who had retired in 1958. One team not on the grid at Kyalami that day was Shadow whose driver Peter Revson had been killed a week earlier in testing for the GP. The team withdrew from the race after the accident.

FIA President Max Mosley was no doubt choking on his cornflakes when he got up and saw the papers today in 2008 when the *News of the World* published their infamous exposé on his private life. The newspaper claimed an orgy he took part in had Nazi overtones. Mosley admitted the orgy with five prostitutes but denied the Nazi theme, took the paper to court and won.

MARCH 31

If many Formula One fans were dismayed by Michael Schumacher's dominance of the sport, the news that he had a younger brother who was also pretty nifty behind the wheel may not have been good. In 1999 Ralf Schumacher joined Williams and by 2001 the Grove team was moving back towards winning ways. Michael and Ralf made history on this day in 2001 when they qualified first and second respectively for the Brazilian Grand Prix. They were the first siblings to achieve a front row lockout in F1 history.

A year later back at Interlagos and Enrique Bernoldi caused chaos when he crashed his Arrows in the Sunday morning practice session. The medical car arrived on the scene and the driver Alex Ribeiro opened his door. At that moment Nick Heidfeld came round the corner in his Sauber and with nowhere to go, took to the grass and smashed into the open door of the Mercedes. A split-second later and Ribeiro might have been killed.

FORMULA ONE
On This Day

APRIL

APRIL 1

In the years before Felipa Massa's arrival in F1 the Brazilian fans only had eyes, ears, air horns and banners for Rubens Barrichello but at the 2001 Brazilian GP held on this day it was a Colombian star that made all the headlines. Making only his third F1 start for Williams, Juan Pablo Montoya soon made his mark on Michael Schumacher by muscling past him at the Senna S, forcing the Ferrari a touch wide in the same way Schumacher has done to countless rivals. Just when he was cruising and looking good for the win Montoya's race was ended when he was rear-ended by Jos Verstappen in the Arrows. Coulthard picked up the pieces and overtook Schumacher with a spectacular move but all the talk was about Montoya, F1's newest star.

Barrichello had a miserable home race – as usual. Rubinho has failed to finish the Brazilian GP eight times and has never won, despite some spirited drives when his machinery often let him down. This year was no different; he collided with Ralf Schumacher on lap two and was out on the spot.

APRIL 2

In 1978 Mario Andretti won most races with Lotus but when he didn't win, Ferrari invariably did. Today in 1978 Carlos Reutemann won the United States Grand Prix West at Long Beach, California for the Prancing Horse team. His teammate Gilles Villeneuve looked to be heading for his first win but he crashed out while trying to pass backmarkers. Reutemann spun as well but survived to win by just ten seconds ahead of title rival Andretti.

Fernando Alonso wrapped up his tenth F1 victory at the Australian Grand Prix in Melbourne today in 2006. He was joined on the podium by Kimi Raikkonen in second and Ralf Schumacher in third – it was the last time the German would ever make it onto the rostrum.

APRIL 3

Mario Andretti became the first American driver to win on home soil in F1 today in 1977 when he triumphed for Lotus in the United States Grand Prix West at Long Beach, California. His popular victory was somewhat fortunate as Jody Scheckter had been leading until the penultimate lap when a deflating tyre caused him to drop to third. Andretti won four races that season but would have to wait until 1978 to win the championship.

On this day in 1988 in Brazil Alain Prost and Ayrton Senna contested their first grand prix as teammates after Ron Dennis had lured the Brazilian to McLaren to form a super team. Typically Senna grabbed pole and also typically Prost was not concerned and saved his energies for the race. In the end he was helped when Senna's car got stuck in first gear ruining his race. Prost drove off into the distance to win but it was Senna who came out on top in the championship that season.

APRIL 4

Having retired in 1979 Niki Lauda decided to return to Formula One in 1982 and secured a drive with McLaren despite misgivings from title sponsor Marlboro about his ability to win after such a break. They needn't have worried and today in 1982 he proved it when he won the USA Grand Prix West at Long Beach, just his third race for the team.

Best poker faces were on today in 2001 when a rival championship to Formula One was announced by Paolo Cantarella, chairman of the European Automobile Manufacturers Association (ACEA). The ACEA represented the major carmakers in F1 who wanted a bigger slice of the TV and commercial earnings from the sport. The rival series announcement was seen by many to be a bluff to force Bernie Ecclestone into making concessions and it never happened.

APRIL 5

Nigel Mansell continued his domination of the season today in 1992 when he took victory in the Brazilian Grand Prix at Interlagos in his lightening-quick Williams-Renault. It was his third win on the trot but he did not have it all his own way and had to battle past teammate Riccardo Patrese after making a poor start.

This race was also the first one British driver Perry McCarthy tried to enter. He had been signed up by the short-lived Andrea Moda team but was denied a super licence and was not even allowed to attempt to qualify. He later achieved fame as *Top Gear's* tame racing driver The Stig until he was sacked for revealing his identity in his autobiography.

APRIL 6

A drama-filled race took place at Interlagos in Brazil on this day in 2003 when heavy rain meant the race was started behind the safety car. The wet weather caused havoc for the drivers. On 54 laps Mark Webber had a terrifying crash in his Jaguar after the final corner leaving debris strewn all over the track. Alonso failed to notice the waved yellows and hurtled round the corner into the wreckage and that crash was enough to see the race red-flagged. Confusion reigned over who had won the GP with Raikkonen initially given the victory by the stewards only for Jordan's Giancarlo Fisichella to be awarded the win several days later.

There was heartbreak in the race for local hero Rubens Barrichello who had secured pole and then survived a bad start to retake a commanding lead. A fuel system fault on lap 47 robbed him of victory as he had to retire. In the other Ferrari Michael Schumacher crashed meaning it was the first time for four years that neither of the red cars finished a race.

APRIL 7

Often described as the most naturally talented British driver ever, Jim Clark was a reserved private man from a farming background. He was World Champion twice, and won 25 of the 72 grands prix he entered. Today in 1968 he was competing in a Formula Two race at Hockenheim when his car went off and hit a tree. He was dead before he got to hospital. His friend and rival Chris Amon said: 'If it could happen to him, what chance did the rest of us have? We all felt that we'd lost our leader.'

Pedro Diniz was not in Clark's class, but he did bring a hefty amount of sponsorship with him thanks to his family's supermarket chain. He is probably most famous for a nasty fire that engulfed his Ligier at the Argentine Grand Prix on this day in 1996. *The Sun* ran the headline 'Diniz in the oven'.

APRIL 8

Gilles Villeneuve never won the World Championship but the closest he came was 1979 when he was second after winning three races. One of those was the USA Grand Prix held on this day which had a farcical start. Having qualified on pole Villeneuve led the field round for the parade lap but overshot his grid shot so decided to take the whole pack around again. When they arrived back on the grid Jacques Laffite's wheels locked up turning him sideways, so Villeneuve led half the field around again for a third parade lap. When the race eventually got started Villeneuve led home Jody Scheckter for a Ferrari 1-2.

The Ferraris were well and truly beaten on this day in 2007 at the Malaysian Grand Prix. After a dominant win for Kimi Raikkonen at the opening round in Australia the red team had expected to be the class of the field again, but were soundly beaten by McLaren with Fernando Alonso and Lewis Hamilton claiming the Woking team's first 1-2 since 2005.

APRIL 9

Today in 1995 Formula One returned to Argentina for the first time in 14 years for a grand prix in Buenos Aires. David Coulthard took his first pole position and might well have secured his first F1 win had his Williams not given up on lap 16. Instead his teammate Damon Hill took his first win of the season after passing Michael Schumacher.

Michael Schumacher has often said the rival he respected most during his time in F1 was Mika Hakkinen. Throughout the late 1990s and early 2000s the two drivers were often locked in battle on the track and today in 2000 at the San Marino GP at Imola was no different. As usual Hakkinen had grabbed pole and made a good start but Schumacher used his trademark trick of staying out for a couple of laps longer than his rival and somehow emerging from the pitstops ahead and in the lead. It was another victory for the German, and Mika had to settle for second.

APRIL 10

Until the 1980s non-championship races were common throughout the year and in the very first F1 season in 1950 two such races were held on this day. The Richmond Trophy was run at the famous Goodwood circuit in England which Reg Parnell won in a Maserati. Meanwhile Juan Manuel Fangio also drove a Maserati to victory on the same day in Pau Grand Prix in France.

As the sport was becoming more regulated and commercial gradually the non-championship races faded out. The 1983 Race of Champions, held on this day at Brands Hatch was the last non-championship Formula One race to be run in the sport's history. Reigning World Champion Keke Rosberg won the race from pole despite a close challenge from Danny Sullivan in his Tyrrell, who was a late call up to race after the team's lead driver Michele Alboreto had to race at another event.

APRIL 11

The great drivers truly show their greatness in the wet. On this day in 1993 perhaps the greatest of them all demonstrated the point with a simply stunning drive in changeable conditions at Donington Park in the European Grand Prix. Ayrton Senna started from fourth on the grid behind Michael Schumacher's Benetton and the Williams of Alain Prost and Damon Hill. The race started with the rain coming down and Senna drove a remarkable opening lap. Wendlinger managed to get past him and Schumi at the start but Senna took the German on the exit of Redgate before getting past Wendlinger on the Craner Curves. He had Hill behind him by Coppice corner and took Prost at the hairpin. Fifth to first in what is remembered as perhaps the best single lap by any driver in the history of F1.

Senna's protégé Rubens Barrichello delighted his home supporters by qualifying third for the Brazilian GP today in 1999 in his Stewart-Ford. He even led for an early part of the race but a car failure would rob him of yet another chance to finish well in his home race as Mika Hakkinen took the win.

APRIL 12

The Argentine Grand Prix was first held in 1953, the brainchild of President Juan Peron who wanted to take advantage of the success of Argentine racing driver Juan Manuel Fangio. He didn't win the first race but did take victory four years on the trot after that. No Argentine driver has taken victory on home soil since then but today in 1981 Carlos Reutemann got agonisingly close when he finished second to Brazilian Nelson Piquet.

The very last Argentine GP also took place on this day in 1998. The McLarens of David Coulthard and Mika Hakkinen were expected to dominate but a clever strategy allowed Michael Schumacher to win for Ferrari.

APRIL 13

The F1 circus arrived at Jerez in 1986 for the first Spanish GP for five years. The race, held on this day, was a corker with a great three-way battle between Senna, Prost and Mansell. The Englishman had started second but slipped to third after Prost overtook him. Then Mansell went on a charge and passed both Prost and Senna to lead by lap 39. Senna came back at Mansell and passed him for the lead with Prost sneaking through to take second at the same time. Mansell then gambled and came in for fresh tyres, coming out a massive 20 seconds off the lead with nine laps left. Nige was lapping four seconds quicker than Senna and quickly overtook Prost. On the last lap Senna and Mansell were neck and neck and Senna just managed to take the win by 0.014 seconds as they crossed the line together. It was the second closest finish in F1 history.

A proud day for Jacques Villeneuve today in 1997 at the Brazilian GP when he won to rack up six Formula One victories and equal his father Gilles' total.

APRIL 14

The most famous and glamorous race in the world is undoubtedly the Monaco Grand Prix, the first of which took place on this day in 1929. It was organised by Anthony Noghes, after whom a corner of the circuit is now named.

The race was won by the mysterious Englishman entered as W Williams. His real name was William Grover-Williams, a British expatriate who had grown up in Monte Carlo. Just like a real-life James Bond, Grover-Williams was not only a grand prix-winning racing driver, but was also a secret agent and worked for British intelligence during World War Two, setting up information networks in occupied France. He was eventually captured by the Nazis and executed in a concentration camp.

APRIL 15

The San Marino Grand Prix at Imola is Ferrari territory but today in 2001 Williams upset the locals by taking the win – the team's first since their championship winning year in 1997 and the first ever win for Ralf Schumacher who upstaged his brother for once and made history in the process – they became the first siblings to each win Formula One grands prix. It was also the first win for Williams' engine partner BMW who took just 21 races to reach the top step of the podium since joining the sport.

From the John Player Special Lotus to Marlboro's long-time affiliation with McLaren and Ferrari, tobacco advertising provided much of the money for teams to go racing until the European Commission banned it in 2005. Today in 2003 the Williams team announced a groundbreaking sponsorship deal with NiQuitin CQ, a range of products to help people give up smoking. Sir Frank Williams said: 'This deal confirms that there is a future for Formula One after tobacco sponsorship.'

APRIL 16

Since the early part of this decade, as the influence of the car manufacturers in F1 increased, they have been demanding a greater share of the profit the series makes. So frustrated were they by Bernie Ecclestone's efforts to deny them this, that they threatened to set up a rival series and pull out of F1. Today in 2002 it seemed like Bernie and his bankers realised they might have to make some concessions and offered the manufacturers a 30 per cent stake in SLEC, the company that controls the sport's commercial rights.

It really was the end of an era for McLaren today in 2009 as Ron Dennis, the boss of the team since 1981, announced he was ending his involvement in the F1 team entirely to concentrate on the road car business. He said: 'I admit I'm not always easy to get on with. I admit I've always fought hard for McLaren in Formula One.'

APRIL 17

Alain Prost delighted his home crowd today when he won the French Grand Prix at Paul Ricard for Renault. It was his second victory on home soil and he would go on to win the event six times – more than any other driver bar Michael Schumacher who won it eight times.

Schumacher was standing on top of the podium on this day in 1994 when he won the Pacific Grand Prix at Aida, Japan. Ayrton Senna had qualified on pole but was then shunted by McLaren's Mika Hakkinen, putting him out of the race. When the teams arrived in Japan for the race rumours were flying around that Schumacher's Benetton might be running some illegal traction control software, although this was strongly denied by the team. After he was shunted out of the race Senna stood at the side of the track watching and listening to Schumacher's car. When asked if he thought Benetton were using traction control he told Lotus team boss Peter Collins: 'I am sure they are.'

APRIL 18

Jackie Stewart won the Spanish GP at Montjuic Park today in 1971. It was his first victory of six that season as he won his second World Championship.

Giancarlo Fisichella missed out on the chance to celebrate his first F1 win on the podium at the Brazilian GP in 2003 after the stewards wrongly credited Kimi Raikkonen with the victory. After protests from Fisi's team Jordan, the powers that be revised their decision and gave the win to the Italian. On this day in 2003 a unique prize giving ceremony took place before the San Marino GP at Imola when Raikkonen handed Fisi the winner's trophy while Ron Dennis handed over the constructors' pot to Eddie Jordan. 'I must be the first F1 driver in history to win his first GP on a Friday and receive the trophy a week later,' said Fisichella.

APRIL 19

These days many F1 stars live in Monte Carlo but there has only ever been one Monaco-born winner of the Monaco Grand Prix. Today in 1931 Louis Chiron took a popular victory in a Bugatti. The Monegasque driver beat Luigi Fagioli (Maserati) and Achille Varzi (Bugatti) to the flag.

Perhaps the most famous and successful of all F1 cars made its debut today in 1970 at the Spanish Grand Prix. The fabled Lotus 72, designed by Colin Chapman and Maurice Philippe first took to the track in the hands of Jochen Rindt but it was an inauspicious start for the car when Rindt lasted just eight laps before an ignition problem forced him to retire. John Miles in the other 72 had failed even to qualify for the race. Despite this start the car won both drivers' and constructors' championships in 1970. Various updates helped the car take both titles again in 1972, and another constructors' title in 1973. The car raced right through to 1975 and when it was finally retired the wedge-shaped wonder had won 20 of its 75 races.

APRIL 20

Michael Schumacher won the San Marino Grand Prix at Imola today in 2003 – normally the cue for unconfined rejoicing for Ferrari and the thousands of fanatical Tifosi but not this time. His closest challenger in the race had been brother Ralf but the two men had only decided to race at the last minute after the death of their mother Elisabeth just hours before the race started. Both brothers wore black armbands and the podium celebrations were muted with no champagne sprayed.

The win was the final race for the highly successful Ferrari F2002 car which had won both titles for the team in 2002 when Michael Schumacher finished first or second in every race bar one, when he finished third. The team introduced their new car at the next race. The F2003-GA won on its debut with Schumi at the wheel.

APRIL 21

Throughout his career Ayrton Senna was feted as a wet weather driver in a league all of his own. How appropriate then that he secured his first ever F1 win in the rain at the Portuguese Grand Prix at Estoril on this day in 1985. In just his second season in the sport Senna took pole and then drove away from the rest of the field who splashed around behind him forlornly. The conditions were so bad that Alain Prost, none too shabby in the wet himself, even spun off on lap 30. A new star had arrived.

Rain was also an important factor today in 2000 when wet weather caused chaos at the British Grand Prix. On this day, the Friday before the race, organisers were forced to close the car parks in the hope of them being usable for race day. It was so wet that a Land Rover sent to tow David Coulthard's McLaren back on to the track became bogged itself.

APRIL 22

Rubens Barrichello mirrored his great mentor Ayrton Senna with his wet weather driving ability and he put it to good use today in 2000 at Silverstone when he grabbed pole position in the rain for Ferrari. Sadly a hydraulics problem forced him to retire while David Coulthard, who started fourth, battled through to win his home race for the second year in succession.

Part of Senna's magic was his amazing ability to get pole position on the grid no matter what car he was driving. Such was his talent that when he was killed he had amassed a record 65 poles, almost double that of his nearest rivals' total with Jim Clark and Alain Prost both on 33. It was a record that looked unbeatable until Michael Schumacher began breaking records like Roy Castle on speed. Today in 2006 Schumi broke Senna's record of 65 pole positions in qualifying for the San Marino GP at Imola.

APRIL 23

With overtaking not as easy as it once was in F1 the qualifying session before a race has become just as key to the outcome as the race itself, and is often just as exciting. In recent years the format of qualifying has been altered more than once but the basic principle remains that whoever sets the fastest lap starts from the front of the grid. It was not always so in the early days when grid positions were decided by ballot. The first grand prix to use qualifying rather than the ballot system was held today in 1933 at Monaco. Achille Varzi won from pole in his Bugatti.

Gerhard Berger started from fifth on this day in 1989 at the San Marino GP but his race lasted just three laps after his car went off at Tamburello corner and smashed into the wall at 180 miles per hour, before bursting into flames. Marshals arrived quickly to put the fire out and Berger sustained burns and a broken rib which kept him out of the next race at Monaco.

APRIL 24

The threat to take F1 from free-to-air terrestrial to pay TV was averted on this day in 2001 when the FIA announced it had signed a 100-year deal for the commercial and broadcasting rights to the sport with Bernie Ecclestone's SLEC organisation. The deal was key in preventing the major car manufacturers from forming their own breakaway championship.

Formula One fans in the UK were cursing ITV's coverage of the San Marino GP on this day in 2005. A thrilling race was heading for a dramatic climax with Fernando Alonso and Michael Schumacher going head to head when, with just three laps left, producers cut to an advertising break. Viewers were dumbfounded and ITV returned to the action just in time to see Alonso win from Schumacher by just 0.21 seconds. Stirling Moss said: 'I can only assume the producer was a football fan.'

APRIL 25

The grid for the San Marino GP at Imola on this day in 1982 was somewhat diminished because of a boycott by some teams as the FISA/FOCA war between the governing body and the teams raged, but that was overshadowed by a huge row between Ferrari teammates Gilles Villeneuve and Didier Pironi. Villeneuve was leading from Pironi and the team ordered them both to slow down to save fuel. Villeneuve thought this meant they were to hold position but on the last lap Pironi overtook him and took victory. Villeneuve was furious at what he perceived as betrayal and vowed never to speak to Pironi again. Tragically he kept his word as the Canadian was killed two weeks later during qualifying for the Belgian Grand Prix at Zolder.

The third man on that uncomfortable podium at Imola was Michele Alboreto, the popular Italian who went on to drive for Ferrari and notched five wins in nearly 200 grands prix. Today in 2001 he was killed while testing an Audi R8 for Le Mans at a track in Germany.

APRIL 26

In 1998 the McLaren-Mercedes was the class of the field but Mika Hakkinen made the most of it winning the championship and taking eight victories. By contrast David Coulthard won just one race, the San Marino Grand Prix at Imola on this day. Having snatched a rare pole position away from Hakkinen, Coulthard made a good start and raced off into the distance while Hakkinen was forced to retire with a gearbox failure.

Ferrari were well beaten on their home turf but Schumacher and Irvine did provide some consolation for the Tifosi by finishing second and third respectively.

APRIL 27

A tragic Spanish GP took place today in 1975 at Montjuic Park. The event had started badly when the drivers went on strike in protest at the poor state of the crash barriers. World Champion Emerson Fittipaldi was so upset he decided not to race and went home. Eventually the barriers were fixed and the race went ahead, but it turned to carnage immediately with no fewer than eight cars involved in crashes. On lap 26 Rolf Stommelen's rear wing failed and his car went flying over a barrier, killing four people.

Fuel was the deciding factor in the San Marino GP at Imola on this day in 1986 when no fewer than five of the runners ran out before the end of the race and had to park up. Keke Rosberg, Riccardo Patrese, Thierry Boutsen, Marc Surer and Piercarlo Ghinzani all succumbed to petrol problems before, on the last lap just three corners from the chequered flag, leader Alain Prost started running out too. He weaved his McLaren this way and that to try to slosh the last remaining drops from the tank into the pipe. He just did enough and took the victory before his car ground to a halt on the straight.

APRIL 28

Damon Hill got a new job today in 2006 when he was elected as the new president of the British Racing Drivers' Club at their annual general meeting. The BRDC, which owns the Silverstone circuit, choose Hill to replace Sir Jackie Stewart. Hill said: 'To be elected to such a prestigious club is an honour. It's a big job.'

Also today in 2006 Dave Richards' Prodrive company was granted permission to enter an F1 team in 2008. Richards had previously served as team boss at Benetton and BAR but his own team has yet to enter the sport after a row over its proposed use of customer cars.

APRIL 29

In 2001 Mika Hakkinen looked a shadow of his former self. With the McLaren no longer the cream of the field and two world titles under his belt the Flying Finn seemed to lack some motivation in the car. On some days, like today, his talent would not be suppressed and at the Spanish GP at Barcelona he outclassed everyone and looked to be heading for his first win of the year when, on the very last lap, his engine gave up. Michael Schumacher inherited a fortuitous win but was apologetic about his victory. He said: 'I went to see him because it's not the way you like to win a race honestly, but then sometimes it happens in racing.'

Michael was joined on the podium by Juan Pablo Montoya and Jacques Villeneuve – the first time two winners of the Indianapolis 500 had been on the rostrum since Graham Hill and Jim Clark in South Africa in 1968.

APRIL 30

The 1994 San Marino Grand Prix was a black weekend for the sport, not only because of the death of Ayrton Senna, but also because the race meeting also took the life of little-remembered Austrian driver Roland Ratzenberger on this day. The 33-year-old was an F1 rookie with the Simtek team. He was killed when his car went off at high speed at the Villeneuve corner during qualifying. It was the first death in the sport since 1982. Damon Hill recounted later how Ayrton Senna had gone to the scene of the accident. He said: 'He came back, very upset and angry, and told us Roland was dead.'

The following month a journalist criticised FIA President Max Mosley for not attending Senna's funeral, as the rest of the F1 world had. Mosley said he had gone to Ratzenberger's funeral instead. 'Roland had been forgotten,' he said. 'So I went to his funeral because everyone went to Senna's. I thought it was important that somebody went to his.'

FORMULA ONE
On This Day

MAY

MAY 1

After Ratzenberger's death and another big crash for Rubens Barrichello most people thought the San Marino GP could not get any worse. They were wrong and on this day, Ayrton Senna, three-time World Champion and arguably the greatest driver the sport had ever seen, was killed when his Williams car went off at high speed at Tamburello and smashed into the wall. The world looked on in horror as the medical team tried in vain to save him. Ironically, Senna had been the driver most moved by the death of Ratzenberger and that very morning before the race he and the other drivers had decided to reform the Grand Prix Drivers' Association to try to improve safety. It fell to Murray Walker to report the news to the British viewers. 'To say that his loss is tragic is a masterpiece of understatement,' he said.

When examining the wreckage of Senna's car track officials discovered a furled Austrian flag inside the cockpit which the Brazilian intended to raise in honour of Ratzenberger if he won the race.

MAY 2

Today in 1976 a truly radical car took to the track for its first race. The Tyrrell P34 six-wheeled F1 car made its debut at the Spanish GP in front of astonished onlookers. It was the first, and only, six-wheeler in the sport. Patrick Depailler qualified the car in third but retired from the race with brake problems on lap 26, but the car raced on for two seasons, even winning the 1976 Swedish GP with Jody Scheckter at the wheel.

Today in 2000 David Coulthard was playing the hero when the private jet he was flying to France in crashed on landing at Lyon-Satolas airport. The Scot, who had won the British GP a few days earlier, helped his girlfriend Heidi Winchelski and his bodyguard escape the burning plane. Sadly the pilot and co-pilot were killed.

MAY 3

Nigel Mansell took victory for Williams-Honda today in the 1987 San Marino Grand Prix at Imola. The Englishman started second on the grid to Senna in the Lotus but soon overtook the Brazilian and drove off into the distance to win by nearly half a minute over Senna. Meanwhile Satoru Nakajima, father of current Williams driver Kazuki, finished sixth for Lotus and became the first Japanese driver to score a Formula One World Championship point.

Mansell was also the victor on this day in 1992 in the Spanish Grand Prix in Barcelona. It was his fourth victory out of four as he steamrollered his way to the title. Perry McCarthy, who would later become The Stig on *Top Gear* fared a little better than his previous F1 outing in Brazil. He had now managed to get a super licence but his Andrea Moda car was not playing ball and in pre-qualifying he managed about ten yards before his engine blew and he was out again.

MAY 4

The F1 field was used to Jackie Stewart racing off into the distance in the sixties and seventies and on this day in 1969 'JYS' won the Spanish Grand Prix at Montjuic Park near Barcelona by the biggest margin ever in an F1 race up to that point. Chris Amon crashed out while leading the race leaving Stewart to inherit the lead. He crossed the finish line a full two laps clear of the second placed man Bruce McLaren.

Frenchman Didier Pironi took his first victory today in 1980, triumphing in a Ligier in the Belgian Grand Prix at Zolder. In an exciting time for the sport he became the third new winner in four races, joining fellow Frenchman Rene Arnoux and Brazilian Nelson Piquet. The race is also notable as the only one contested by television presenter Tiff Needell who drove for Ensign but retired on lap 23 with engine failure.

MAY 5

Thomas Scheckter, son of 1979 World Champion Jody, was in a spot of bother on this day in 2001 when he was sacked from his job as test driver for the Jaguar team after he was caught kerb-crawling in Milton Keynes.

In 2002 the Prost team was dying a slow death with debts forcing the owner Alain Prost to wind up the team. On this day that year 12 of the Prost team cars were sold at auction at the Palais de Congres in Paris. The sale raised just $900,000.

MAY 6

Ayrton Senna was the supreme one-lap specialist and a pole position expert. He achieved 65 pole positions in his Formula One career, an amazing statistic bettered only by Michael Schumacher on 68, although Schumi had nearly 100 more races to set his record. The San Marino GP today in 1984 is unique in that it is the only race Senna failed to qualify for. A dispute between his Toleman team and the Pirelli tyre company meant he could not run in the first session and an engine problem robbed him of his chance in the second.

In the race Senna's great rival Alain Prost took the victory in his McLaren-TAG Porsche as the Brazilian could only look on.

MAY 7

Ferrari's Italian driver Lorenzo Bandini qualified on the front row of the grid for the Monaco GP on this day in 1967 and was running second when he crashed at the chicane and his car rolled over and caught fire. He was trapped underneath the burning wreckage and marshals had to right his car before pulling his unconscious body out. He died three days later from his injuries. He said once: 'I think life is all fate, it's not only a man driving a car. If you have to go, if it is written your time is that day, you will die whether you go racing or not.'

Since 1992 his family have awarded the Lorenzo Bandini Trophy to an outstanding figure from the world of racing. Fellow Italian Ivan Capelli was the first recipient.

MAY 8

Frank Williams' first attempt at being a team owner was not successful and in 1976 Canadian millionaire Walter Wolf bought him out and then sacked him from the team. Undeterred Frank tried again and today in 1977 at the Spanish GP at Jarama, Williams Grand Prix Engineering Ltd debuted with Patrick Neve driving a March car. He finished 12th, four laps down. Two years later the team won its first race.

Yet another tragedy occurred on this day in 1982 in qualifying for the Belgian Grand Prix at Zolder when Gilles Villeneuve was killed. The Ferrari driver, still furious with teammate Pironi after their dispute at Imola two weeks earlier, went out to try to take pole position but hit the rear of Jochen Mass's car which sent Villeneuve's car cartwheeling through the air. Gilles was thrown from the car into fencing. The first two drivers on the scene, Derek Warwick and John Watson pulled up to help their friend, but he was pronounced dead later that day. F1 had been robbed of one of the sport's most charismatic drivers whose exciting style had made him a crowd favourite.

MAY 9

Today in 1982 the Belgian Grand Prix went ahead despite the death of Gilles Villeneuve in qualifying the day before. His team Ferrari had decided not to race so Didier Pironi was also out. In their absence John Watson won the race for McLaren, followed by Keke Rosberg for Williams. Niki Lauda finished third but was later disqualified for his car being underweight so his place went to Eddie Cheever.

The Spanish Grand Prix has been held twice on this day. First in 1993, when Alain Prost won in his Williams-Renault from his nemesis Ayrton Senna in the McLaren-Ford.

In the 2004 event Michael Schumacher won for Ferrari but there was confusion on the parade lap when a well-known Catalan pitch invader called Jimmy Jump ran on to the track. The man who has also invaded the Euro 2004 football final and various other European Cup and La Liga matches was swiftly removed.

MAY 10

Team orders has always been a contentious subject in motor racing. Usually the object is to ensure a particular driver wins the race or the title but on this day in 1936 the object of team orders at the Tripoli Grand Prix went beyond motor racing to international diplomacy. The fascist governments of Germany and Italy were seeking to form an alliance so orders had been sent to the dominant Auto Union team that German drivers should win on German soil and Italians in Italy. Germany's Hans Stuck was leading the race when team boss Karl Feuereissen told him to slow down and told Italian Achille Varzi to speed up. Both obeyed and Varzi caught Stuck unawares on the last lap to win the race from the German.

Later at the victory party Varzi was humiliated when Marshal Balbo, leader of Italian North Africa, proposed a toast to Stuck, 'the real winner'.

MAY 11

Ferrari is undoubtedly the biggest name in motor racing now but in the beginning Enzo Ferrari ran the factory racing team for Alfa Romeo. After World War Two the Old Man decided to build his own cars and today in 1947 the first car to bear the Ferrari name entered a race at the Piacenza circuit in northern Italy. The Tipo 125 S showed well and led the race until a fuel pump problem two laps from the finish ended its race. The greatest motor racing story had begun.

Rubens Barrichello was a loyal servant to Ferrari for many years, serving as deputy to Michael Schumacher. Today in 2008 at the Turkish Grand Prix Rubinho became the most experienced driver in F1 history having contested more grands prix than any other driver.

MAY 12

The McLaren team was mourning the loss of Paul Morgan who died today in 2001. Morgan founded Illmor with Mario Illien and the company built Mercedes F1 engines for the McLaren team. Morgan died when his light aircraft crashed.

Today in 2002 one of the most controversial races of recent times took place at the A1-Ring in Austria. Having dominated qualifying and the race, Rubens Barrichello was ordered to yield for teammate Michael Schumacher, which he did on the final lap, much to the disgust of the crowd who booed throughout the podium ceremony. Schumacher tried to push Rubens on to the top step but the damage was done. Both the blatant use of team orders and the podium debacle earned Ferrari the displeasure of the FIA who fined them $500,000 and banned team orders. In November 2008 Barrichello claimed he had been threatened with the sack on the last lap if he did not allow Schumacher through. He said: 'I was told to think about my contract. For me that was an order: it is better for you to lift your foot, otherwise you are going to be going home.'

MAY 13

The first ever F1 World Championship kicked off today in 1950 when the field competed at Silverstone for the British GP in front of King George VI and Queen Elizabeth. The Alfa Romeos were dominant and Giuseppe Farina won after Fangio went out with engine trouble eight laps from the finish. Farina went on to win the inaugural world title.

Forty years later to the day and Nigel Mansell was displaying some of the fighting spirit in his Ferrari that led the Tifosi to nickname him 'Il Leone' in the San Marino GP of 1990. Having qualified fifth on the grid behind both McLarens and Williamses, Nigel began fighting his way through the field. After problems for Pirro, Senna and Boutsen, Mansell found himself second to Gerhard Berger and on lap 36 he tried to take the lead at Tamburello. He was forced onto the grass which caused him to spin dramatically. Nigel managed to regain control of the car and set off in pursuit once more before engine gremlins forced him to retire. Riccardo Patrese won the race.

MAY 14

Murray Walker has been synonymous with motor racing and particularly Formula One for longer than anyone can remember. On this day in 1949 Murray did his first grand prix commentary when the BBC asked him to cover the second position at Stowe Corner at Silverstone for the British Grand Prix. He got the gig after impressing BBC bosses with his commentary at the Shelsley Walsh hill-climb event in Worcestershire, when he stepped in at the last minute to cover for his father. He obviously cut the mustard and was still there more than half a century later screaming inaccuracies at us.

Sir Stirling Moss drove one of the greatest races of his career today in 1961 when he won the Monaco Grand Prix in a Lotus-Climax despite a huge power disadvantage to the Ferraris of Richie Ginther, Phil Hill and Wolfgang Von Trips who all finished behind him.

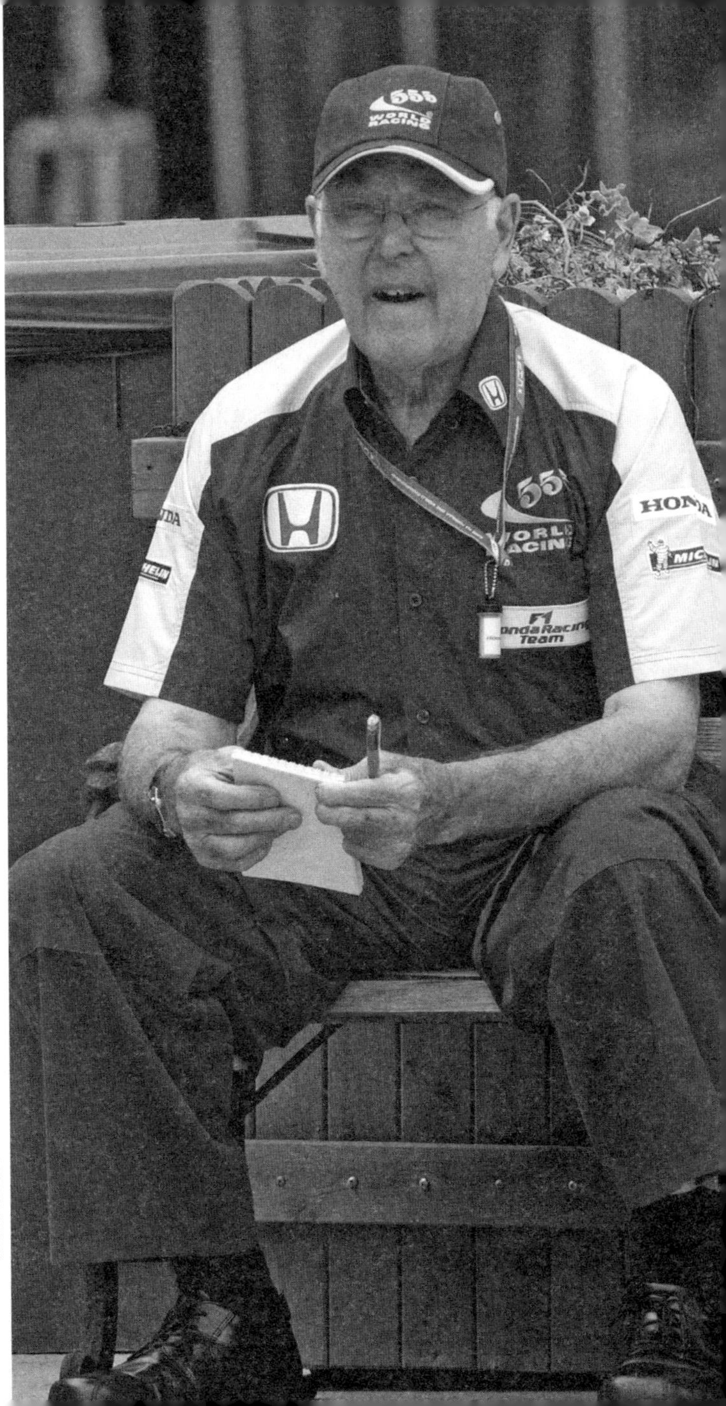

MURRAY WALKER

MAY 15

After the deaths of Roland Ratzenberger and Ayrton Senna two weeks earlier, the teams assembled for the Monaco GP in a sombre mood and with the world's media watching on this day in 1994. To add to the air of foreboding Karl Wendlinger had a massive crash during Thursday practice which put him in a coma and led to the Sauber-Mercedes team abandoning the meeting. On race day the drivers held a minute's silence before the start and the two front row grid positions were left clear and painted with the colours of the Brazilian and Austrian flags. In the race itself Damon Hill and Mika Hakkinen had a coming together which put them both out leaving Michael Schumacher to take the win ahead of Martin Brundle and Gerhard Berger.

Before Senna and Ratzenberger the last man to be killed in an F1 car was Italian Elio de Angelis. He was called F1's last gentleman racer as he was from a wealthy background and could play the piano to concert standard but today in 1986 he was killed while testing for Lotus at the Paul Ricard track in France. His close friend Nigel Mansell watched it happen. He said: 'Alain Prost and I tried to get him out but the car was crackling and exploding and there was just no way. Poor Elio had no chance.'

MAY 16

Two Ferrari 1-2s have occurred on this day, nearly 30 years apart. The first was at Zolder in 1976 at the Belgian GP when Niki Lauda led home Clay Regazzoni in a race that was more notable for a lucky escape for Chris Amon. A wheel came off his Ensign which crashed and was flipped upside-down but Amon walked away unharmed.

The second was at the 1999 Monaco GP when Eddie Irvine followed his team leader Michael Schumacher to make the top two steps of the podium all red.

MAY 17

Mixed fortunes for Nigel Mansell on this day. In 1987 at the Belgian Grand Prix at Spa-Francorchamps Mansell and Senna tangled as the Englishman tried to overtake the Lotus driver, but the move put them both out. A furious Mansell blamed Senna and stormed down to the Lotus garage to have words. He said: 'I went over to him, grabbed him by the overalls and pushed him up against the wall. He wore loose overalls in those days and I pulled the zip up beyond his chin to just below his nose. "Next time you do that," I said, "You're going to have to do a much better job."'

Five years later to the day and Mansell was celebrating after winning the 1992 San Marino GP. It was his fifth victory out of five races for the season and it meant he broke the record for successive wins at the start of the season, which had been four, set by Senna in 1991.

MAY 18

Bernie Ecclestone is the undisputed king of Formula One. He walks around the paddock, Napoleon-like in stature and power as he rules the sport like his kingdom. But how good a driver is he? Not brilliant if his one dalliance with F1 racing is anything to go by. In 1957 he was managing the Welsh driver Stuart Lewis-Evans and he also bought the Connaught F1 team. He even tried to qualify one of the cars himself for the Monaco GP held today in 1958. Unfortunately he did not make the cut and thereafter concentrated on team and driver management.

In contrast to Bernie, Mika Hakkinen was something of a qualifying specialist but today in 2008 he was in mourning after a fire at his mansion in France destroyed much of the building and claimed the life of his pet tortoise Caroline. No one else was injured and the fire was traced to a faulty light in one of his trophy cabinets.

MAY 19

Monaco seems to throw up dramas and surprises like no other race and today in 1996 saw one of the most incredible grands prix of modern times. On a rain soaked day Michael Schumacher crashed out before Damon Hill, who had a commanding lead, retired with engine trouble. Jean Alesi was leading until his rear suspension failed. As almost every other driver had problems it fell to Olivier Panis, who had started 14th on the grid, to carve his way through the chaos for an unexpected and unbelievable first win in his Ligier. He was the first French driver to win at Monaco in a French car since Rene Dreyfus in a Bugatti in 1930.

Just three cars actually crossed the finish line to complete the race – the fewest number of finishers ever in a modern grand prix, with McLaren's David Coulthard and Sauber's Johnny Herbert completing the podium. Heinz-Harald Frentzen, Mika Salo and Mika Hakkinen were also classified in the points despite not finishing.

MAY 20

Graham Hill graduated to Formula One in 1958 but it was not until today in 1962 at the Dutch Grand Prix at Zandvoort that he finally got his first win. He had qualified second but Jim Clark got ahead of him at the start. When Clark went out with a clutch problem Hill assumed the lead and held on to it until the end. It was one of four wins for him that season as he won his first World Championship.

The Belgian Grand Prix at Zolder on this day in 1973 almost didn't happen at all. The race organisers had surfaced the track late and when the cars began running in Friday practice parts of it were breaking up. The drivers threatened to strike if it was not sorted out so it was hurriedly resurfaced overnight. This solved the problem and Jackie Stewart took the victory on the way to this third and final title.

MAY 21

The second World Championship event of the inaugural season was held on this day in 1950 at Monaco, just eight days after the opening round at Silverstone. The race was notable for a huge pile-up on the first lap when a wave from the harbour flooded the track at Tabac Corner. Nine cars were eliminated at a stroke but Juan Manuel Fangio was able to avoid the carnage and led home the remaining seven cars to win his first World Championship race and his first Monaco victory.

Fangio's fellow Argentine Carlos Reutemann could only manage third place today in 1978 at the Belgian GP at Zolder. As usual for the 1978 season the Lotus team had it all their own way and Mario Andretti led home Ronnie Peterson for a 1-2.

MAY 22

Alberto Ascari took the headlines after the Monaco GP on this day in 1955 despite not winning or even finishing the race. On lap 81 Stirling Moss, leading in his Mercedes, suffered an engine blow-up and Ascari inherited the lead. Unfortunately it didn't last long as he lost control of his Lancia at the chicane and went straight through the hay bales and sandbags into the harbour. He had to swim for the nearest yacht and spent the night in hospital while his car had to be craned out of 25 feet of water. Frenchman Maurice Trintignant took the win in a Ferrari.

Today in 1961 Wolfgang von Trips won the Dutch Grand Prix at Zandvoort for Ferrari. The race is unique in that there were no pitstops and not a single retirement and for decades it was the only race where every single car finished. The 2005 Italian Grand Prix at Monza is the only other race where the full field of drivers all saw the chequered flag.

MAY 23

Another one of those extraordinary races at Monaco today in 1982 when it seemed like no one wanted to win. Pole man Rene Arnoux spun on lap 14 but Prost was leading until rain started on lap 74 and he crashed. Riccardo Patrese was then leading but he spun and stalled at Loews hairpin. Didier Pironi then led but he ran out of fuel going into the tunnel. Andrea de Cesaris would have taken the lead but he too ran out of fuel before the next man in line, Derek Daly, stopped with a gearbox problem. James Hunt commentating said: 'We've got this ridiculous situation we are all sitting by the start/finish line waiting for a winner to come past and we don't seem to be getting one.' Patrese eventually emerged to take the flag, having managed to bump start his car after his spin. Murray Walker described it as: 'Certainly the most eventful, exciting, momentous grand prix I have ever seen.'

At the 2004 Monaco GP also on this day, Christian Klien had a rather costly crash in his Jaguar. A £140,000 diamond was embedded in the nose cone as part of a sponsorship deal. When the team recovered the car after Klien's crash at Loews, it was minus the jewel, which had mysteriously disappeared.

MAY 24

Mika Hakkinen made it a clean sweep at the Monaco GP today in 1998 taking the hat-trick of pole position, fastest lap and the win.

The smaller teams are always trying to gain an edge in Formula One and today in 2001 the Arrows and Jordan teams left their garages to start the Thursday practice session for the Monaco GP amid gasps from onlookers. Both teams had arrived with bizarre-looking extra front-wing attachments designed to give them extra front downforce. The FIA banned them immediately on the grounds of safety but perhaps also out of embarrassment, so ridiculous did they look.

MAY 25

After Elio de Angelis was killed while testing a Brabham at Paul Ricard, the team decided to race with just one car at the next race, the Belgian Grand Prix, held today in 1986. Nigel Mansell was a former teammate of de Angelis and actually witnessed his death but he managed to overcome his emotion to win the race for Williams ahead of Ayrton Senna and Stefan Johansson.

On this day in 2008 the new British hero Lewis Hamilton took victory in the Monaco Grand Prix – he was the first Englishman to win the prestigious event since Graham Hill in 1969. Hamilton survived a puncture and rain to storm though to a great victory while many of the other drivers spun off in the wet conditions.

MAY 26

Just four days after surviving his unscheduled dip in the Monaco harbour Alberto Ascari arrived at Monza where Eugenio Castellotti was testing a Ferrari sports car they would both be using in an upcoming race. Ascari decided he wanted a go, but had not brought his lucky blue helmet with him, so borrowed Castellotti's. On the third lap he crashed and was killed with the reason a complete mystery. The whole of Italy mourned as the eerie similarities between his death and that of his father Antonio became clear. Both died on the 26th day of the month, aged 36 and both drove car number 26. Both had won 13 grands prix and both died four days after surviving previous accidents. They both left a wife and two children.

The fallout from Lola Cars' heroic failure in Formula One continued today in 1997 when the company went into administration after 39 years as a result of the doomed F1 project. The F1 team had competed in just two events in 1997, the Australian and Brazilian Grands Prix, failing to qualify for either of them.

MAY 27

Michael Schumacher won yet again at Monaco today in 2001 to join Graham Hill as a five-time winner on the circuit but he was helped by a failing launch control system on David Coulthard's McLaren. The Scot qualified brilliantly on pole but his car did not move off the line at the start, putting him to the back of the grid. He spent 34 laps behind the slow Arrows car of Enrique Bernoldi, unable to pass him. The young Brazilian was under no obligation to move over for Coulthard, but the Scotsman was not impressed. He said: 'He was trying to wallow in some kind of glory by holding me up. The sporting gesture would have been to pull over but he kept turning across me. He's not a man, he's an idiot.'

The race also saw the first podium for the Jaguar team with Eddie Irvine taking third behind Schumacher and Barrichello. Irv the Swerve said: 'We have two Ferraris and a Jaguar on the podium – that's what motor racing is all about.'

MAY 28

Michael Schumacher took his second consecutive Monaco GP victory today in 1995. The race was red-flagged on the first lap following a big collision between Jean Alesi, David Coulthard and Gerhard Berger but after the re-start Schumacher used a trademark good strategy to win from Damon Hill's Williams. This was also the last grand prix for the Simtek team which folded soon afterwards.

A less successful Monaco GP for Schumacher on this day in 2006 when he had to start from the back of the grid – punishment from the stewards after they adjudged him to have 'parked' his car on the track in qualifying in order to block Fernando Alonso and stop him beating Schumacher's time. In his last ever Monaco GP Schumi fought his way up to fifth but missed out on the chance to equal Senna's record of six wins in the principality.

MAY 29

The FIA had reacted to the deaths of Roland Ratzenberger and Ayrton Senna at Imola by hastily introducing new regulations designed to improve safety and the Spanish GP on this day in 1994 was the first to be affected. David Coulthard made his F1 debut as Ayrton Senna's replacement at Williams as the team tried to pick itself up. Damon Hill now had to step up to the plate as team leader and he duly delivered by winning the race – Williams' first win of the season and the first since Senna's death. On the slowing down lap Damon drove round waving a Union Jack flag he had been given by a marshal.

Damon's day could have been spoilt by Michael Schumacher who had taken pole and looked to be on course for victory until a gearbox failure meant his car was stuck in fifth. Incredibly he managed to keep going, even making a pitstop without stalling to take second.

MAY 30

The 1965 Monaco GP had a reduced field because of a clash with the Indianapolis 500 and both Jim Clark and Dan Gurney elected to race in the American event. The Lotus team also withdrew because of a dispute with the organisers. Despite dropping down to fifth at one point, Monaco specialist Graham Hill fought back to take his third victory in the principality. On lap 79 Paul Hawkins spun at the chicane and went into the harbour – only the second time this has ever happened after Ascari in 1955.

Graham Hill also took victory at the Indianapolis 500 on this day in 1966 as one of just four non-Americans in the 33-man field. Jim Clark came second but many people believe the Scotsman was robbed of victory because the officials missed one of Clark's laps because he spun twice during the race. He thought he had won but it was Hill who got to drink the famous victory milk sparking protests from Clark and his team boss Colin Chapman.

MAY 31

When Jim Clark missed the Monaco GP in 1965 he chose instead to compete in the Indy 500. Clark compensated for missing Monaco by storming to victory at the American event in his Lotus-Ford, beating second-placed man Parnelli Jones by two minutes. It was Ford's first victory in the event.

Nigel Mansell finished second three times in the World Championship but by 1992 there was no stopping him. He won the first five races of the season and so very nearly won the sixth at Monaco on this day. After qualifying on pole and leading almost the whole race he had to make an extra pitstop and emerged behind Ayrton Senna who fended him off to take the win despite constant pressure from the Englishman who weaved and bobbed trying to find a way past the slower McLaren. Murray Walker commentating said: 'I do not see how Mansell, *even* Nigel Mansell on fresh tyres is going to be able to get by.' He couldn't and Senna took his fifth Monaco win.

FORMULA ONE
On This Day

JUNE

JUNE 1

In the nineties there was really only one man all the teams wanted to ensure them success, and he wasn't even a driver. Aerodynamicist and designer Adrian Newey was responsible for the design of the cars that won six drivers' titles between 1992 and 1999 first with Williams and then McLaren. Martin Brundle once said: 'If I was doing my Fantasy F1, and I could only afford Newey or Schumacher, then I would have Newey.' Today in 2001 it was announced that Newey was to move to Jaguar Racing the following year after his McLaren contract expired. It was a major coup for the team but it never actually happened after McLaren boss Ron Dennis persuaded Newey to stay with the Woking team.

Today in 2003 Juan Pablo Montoya won the Monaco Grand Prix for Williams and joined Graham Hill as only the second driver in history to have won the Indianapolis 500 and the Monaco Grand Prix.

JUNE 2

The 1991 Williams-Renault car was undoubtedly fast but it also had reliability problems and Ayrton Senna won the first four races of the season in his McLaren. For the Canadian GP at Montreal things finally looked to be going Williams' way when Nigel Mansell took the lead early on and began racing away into the distance. Senna, Berger and Prost all retired with mechanical problems and going into the last lap Mansell began waving to the crowd, already celebrating in anticipation of his victory. He had tempted fate and with less than a mile to the finish, he had gearbox problems and his car stopped. Riccardo Patrese gratefully inherited the win.

Today in 1996 at the Spanish GP in Barcelona Michael Schumacher had his 'Senna at Donington' moment. In sopping wet conditions which caught out many drivers including championship leader Damon Hill, Schumacher was sublime and serenely drove his Ferrari home to victory, setting a fastest lap 2.2 seconds faster than anyone else. The rain master reigned in Spain.

JUNE 3

Today in 1984 one of the wettest and most contentious grands prix ever was held at Monaco. Nigel Mansell overtook pole-sitter Prost for the lead but then spun out, while Ayrton Senna, in only his seventh GP, announced his arrival to the world with a stunning drive that would have seen him win the race had it not been stopped after 32 laps with the conditions too bad. Prost took the victory.

Race director Jacky Ickx was accused of stopping the race to ensure Prost won but the post script to the race did not come until the end of the season. As the Monaco race had been stopped before 75 per cent of the race distance, only half points were awarded, netting Prost four-and-a-half for his win. Had the race continued and Senna passed him, he would still have picked up six points for second. At the last race of the season Prost lost the championship to Niki Lauda by just half a point.

JUNE 4

The most famous F1 engine of all time made its debut today in 1967 at the Dutch GP at Zandvoort. The Cosworth DFV engine made its F1 bow in the Lotus cars of Graham Hill and Jim Clark. It was an immediate success; Hill qualified on pole but Clark won the race and a new era had arrived in the sport. The engine was made available as a customer unit and suddenly any team could have a fast, powerful and reliable engine for very little cost. The DFV engine took 155 GP victories, 12 drivers' championships and was still racing in F1 15 years after its winning debut.

Ayrton Senna started from pole position for the United States GP at Phoenix today in 1989. It was his 34th pole position, beating Jim Clark's record of 33. He eventually notched up 65 before he was killed.

JUNE 5

Today in 1977 Swiss speedster Gunnar Nilsson won the Belgian Grand Prix at Zolder in a Lotus-Cosworth in wet/dry conditions. It was his only Formula One victory as later in the year he was diagnosed with cancer. In an era when many of his contemporaries died at the wheel of their racing cars, Nilsson succumbed to cancer in October 1978.

On this day in 1983 popular Italian driver Michele Alboreto won the United States Grand Prix in Detroit. Although no one knew it at the time it was a historic result as it was the last ever victory for the Tyrrell team which had powered Jackie Stewart to three drivers' titles in the 1970s.

JUNE 6

The Le Mans 24 Hours disaster of 1955 in which more than 80 spectators were killed after one of the Mercedes in the race flew into the crowd, remains the worst catastrophe in the history of motorsport. One of its consequences was the banning of motor racing in Switzerland. Today in 2007 the Swiss parliament finally voted 97 to 77 to lift the ban.

These dangers were highlighted again on this day in 1960 at the Dutch Grand Prix at Zandvoort. Jack Brabham won the race for Cooper but the result was overshadowed by an accident involving American driver Dan Gurney. The brakes on his BRM car failed and he crashed at the hairpin and a spectator was killed.

JUNE 7

The Gilles Villeneuve Circuit in Montreal is notorious for crashes and comings together at the first corner and the race on this day in 1998 was one of the more spectacular examples. Alex Wurz in his first full season with Benetton tried a banzai move on Jean Alesi's Sauber at the first corner. Wurz hit Alesi and the Austrian's car was pitched into a dramatic barrel roll across the track onto the gravel trap. He collected not only Alesi but also Johnny Herbert in the other Sauber and Jarno Trulli in a Prost. No one was hurt but the race was red flagged and Wurz joined the restarted grid in the spare Benetton.

When the race did restart, there was yet another crash at the first corner, and unbelievably it involved two of the men in the first incident. Ralf Schumacher spun his Jordan just after turn one, causing havoc for the rest of the field including Jarno Trulli and Jean Alesi. The pair tangled and Trulli's car ended up with its rear wheels perched on top of Alesi's car, just inches from his head.

JUNE 8

The Swedish Grand Prix at Anderstorp on this day in 1975 would mark the high point in a promising young driver's career that was cut tragically short soon afterwards. Tony Brise finished sixth for the fledgling Hill team run by Graham Hill. He was killed later that year in the plane crash that also killed Hill and other key members of the team.

Lewis Hamilton looked odds-on for another victory at the Canadian Grand Prix today in 2008 when he made an astonishing mistake and ran into Kimi Raikkonen's Ferrari in the pit lane. With two of the front runners out, Robert Kubica made hay and took his first ever victory, and the first for BMW Sauber. Nick Heidfeld came in second making it a 1-2 finish for the German-Swiss team.

JUNE 9

The McLaren team is one of the most successful F1 outfits in the sport's history and today in 1968 at the Belgian GP at Spa the team achieved its first victory with founder Bruce McLaren at the wheel. The New Zealander had fought his way up through the field and thought he had finished second when he crossed the line. Unbeknown to him Jackie Stewart had made a late pitstop so McLaren had won and he didn't even realise. He said afterwards: 'Cyril Atkins, BRM's chief mechanic, ran up talking excitedly about Jackie Stewart's late pitstop, and saying "what a finish!" I was puzzled. "You crossed the line number one," he said. And then he shouted "You've won! Didn't you know?" I didn't. It's about the nicest thing I've ever been told.'

South African Jody Scheckter was also celebrating on this day in 1974 when he took his first F1 victory at the Swedish GP at Anderstorp.

JUNE 10

After taking his first pole position on the Saturday, on this day in 2007 Lewis Hamilton took his maiden victory in the Canadian GP at the Gilles Villeneuve Circuit and became Britain's 19th grand prix winner. He showed great composure and concentration for a rookie to win a challenging race beset with crashes and safety cars. 'I've been ready for this for quite some time, ready for the win – it was just a matter of where and when,' Hamilton said afterwards.

While one of the young guns of the sport was taking his first win, another new charger was having a more difficult day. Highly-rated Polish driver Robert Kubica had an enormous accident while trying to overtake Jarno Trulli. Kubica's BMW appeared to touch the rear of Trulli's Toyota and the Pole was sent hurtling first into the right hand wall, before rolling back across the track into the opposite wall. He miraculously escaped with no injuries.

JUNE 11

The worst disaster in motor racing history occurred today in 1955 when more than 80 spectators were killed at the Le Mans 24 Hours race in France. A Mercedes driven by Pierre Levegh was flipped into the grandstand after clipping another car on the straight. Levegh was killed instantly. Mercedes immediately withdrew from the race and did not compete in motorsport again until 1987. The race was allowed to continue and most fans in other parts of the track were unaware of the tragedy until afterwards.

One of the most popular grand prix victories of all time occurred today in 1995 when Frenchman Jean Alesi took his only victory in F1 on his 31st birthday, at the Canadian GP in the French-speaking city of Montreal. Alesi took the win in the red number 27 Ferrari which was famously driven by Canadian hero Gilles Villeneuve, after whom the circuit in Montreal is named. The win was a touch fortunate for Jean as gearbox problems dropped Michael Schumacher from the lead to fifth late on. Alesi ran out of fuel on the slowing down lap and Schumacher stopped to give him a lift back to the pits on the back of his car.

JUNE 12

Sir Jackie Stewart was a pioneering champion of improving safety in a sport where serious injuries and deaths were common when he was a driver. Today in the 1966 Belgian GP at Spa JYS came perilously close to losing his own life when a huge rainstorm caused seven of the drivers to crash on the first lap. Stewart was one of them and found himself trapped in his upturned car with a broken shoulder, a cracked rib, internal bruising and covered in petrol. Graham Hill stopped to help him and he luckily escaped before the car caught fire.

Footage from some of the practice sessions for this race was used in the 1966 film *Grand Prix* starring James Garner.

JUNE 13

Jody Scheckter achieved a unique feat on this day at the 1976 Swedish Grand Prix at the Scandinavian Raceway when he became the only man to win a Formula One race in a six-wheeled car. The Tyrrell P34 had made its debut to gasps from the public and other teams alike earlier in the season. Scheckter led home Patrick Depailler in the second P34 to cap a remarkable 1-2 finish for the remarkable-looking car – it's only win.

Barely a month after Gilles Villeneuve was killed the F1 circus arrived at the Montreal circuit that had been renamed in his honour for the Canadian GP today in 1982. Villeneuve's nemesis Didier Pironi was on pole but stalled on the grid and young Italian Riccardo Paletti, in only his second F1 race, slammed into the back of the motionless Ferrari. As Pironi and Professor Sid Watkins, the F1 doctor, were trying to get Paletti out the car burst into flames. He died in hospital from his injuries.

JUNE 14

The story of the Belgian Grand Prix at Spa on this day in 1964 is one of fuel – or the lack of it. As the race was just about to reach its climax Dan Gurney's Brabham ran out of fuel just as he was about to pass Bruce McLaren. Graham Hill's BRM soon followed suit leaving McLaren with a clear path to victory… until his engine also cut out with just a couple of corners to go, having run out of fuel. He coasted towards the finish line willing his car to get there as Jim Clark arrived at full pelt. In a nail-biting finish Clark was able to whiz across the line just before McLaren could get there.

At the Canadian GP today in 1992 Nigel Mansell could not blame fuel problems for his failure to win. In the dominant Williams car he had already won five races that season but spun early on to hand victory to McLaren's Gerhard Berger.

JUNE 15

James Hunt was the original playboy racing driver who lived as fast as he drove and enjoyed speed, women, alcohol and drugs in excess and famously wore a badge on his overalls that read *Sex – Breakfast of Champions*. Hunt the Shunt was also famed for his accidents and he once nearly drowned after he crashed his Formula Ford and ended up in the middle of a lake. Hunt died on this day in 1993 aged just 45. It was not one of his high-speed crashes that did it, but a heart attack which came just hours after he had proposed to his girlfriend Helen.

The 1997 season was shaping up nicely for Olivier Panis. After six races he was third in the championship and going so well in his Prost that he was even a tip for the race win at the Canadian GP, held on this day. Sadly, the day ended badly for the Frenchman when he had a huge accident in the closing stages. The whole of the front of his car was ripped off and he broke both his legs. He was out for seven races but did return to his seat for the final three rounds of the season.

JUNE 16

By 1999 former World Champion Damon Hill was no longer enjoying F1 and he announced on this day that he would be hanging up his helmet at the end of the season. He said: 'Formula One has afforded me many incredible opportunities and I will cherish some fantastic memories. I have fulfilled my ambitions and consider myself very fortunate to have done so.'

One of Damon's fellow British F1 champions was celebrating today in 2001 when he was awarded a knighthood. From now on it would be Sir Jackie Stewart after the three-time World Champion was rewarded for his achievements and his work to improve safety in the sport which claimed the lives of many of his friends.

JUNE 17

There is probably only one F1 car in the history of the sport that has a 100 per cent winning record. The car that holds that unlikely distinction is also one of the unlikeliest ever to take to the track. Along with the Tyrrell P34 six-wheeler, the Brabham BT46B known as the 'Fan Car' was one of the most unusual-looking cars ever built. It was designed by Gordon Murray in an effort to match the dominant ground effect Lotus 79 and it featured a giant fan on the rear of the car which created a partial vacuum under the car. It won its debut race today in 1978 at the Swedish GP in the hands of Niki Lauda and rival teams immediately complained about the legality of the machine. The result was allowed to stand but Brabham owner Bernie Ecclestone withdrew the car before it was outlawed and it was never raced again.

Following Robert Kubica's heavy crash in Canada, Sebastian Vettel took his race seat for the following race on this day in 2007, the United States Grand Prix. He finished eighth to become the youngest ever Formula One points scorer, aged 19 years and 349 days.

JUNE 18

This day has been kind to American racers in F1 history: Phil Hill won the Belgian GP in 1961 today for Ferrari on his way to becoming the first ever American Formula One champion.

There was another American victor in the Belgian GP in 1967 too. This time Dan Gurney triumphed, just two weeks after winning the Le Mans 24 Hours race for Ford. Gurney took victory in his Eagle-Weslake car – it was the first win for an American driver in an American car with an American engine in the history of the sport and the first and last victory for the Eagle team.

JUNE 19

Before Imola in 1994 the Belgian GP at Spa on this day in 1960 was the blackest weekend in F1 history when two drivers were killed in the race. Londoner Chris Bristow tangled with Willy Mairesse's Ferrari on lap 17. His car was thrown into trackside fencing and Bristow was decapitated. Just five laps later Lotus driver Alan Stacey was hit in the face by a bird. He crashed, was thrown from his car and killed.

The most ridiculous grand prix of modern times was staged today in 2005 at the United States GP at Indianapolis when a problem with the Michelin tyres meant the teams running the French tyres could not take the fast-banked turn 13 at speed after Ralf Schumacher suffered a huge crash after his tyre failed. A compromise of installing a temporary chicane before the corner was rejected and all 14 Michelin cars pulled out, leaving just six runners in the race. Michael Schumacher won the farcical event as the 130,000-strong crowd booed throughout.

JUNE 20

Although Bernie Ecclestone is the undisputed king of Formula One, he doesn't actually make or enforce the rules. That task falls to the Fédération Internationale de l'Automobile (FIA). It is a non-profit organisation that oversees all motorsport and represents the interests of motorists all over the world. The forerunner to the FIA was the Association Internationale des Automobile Clubs Reconnus (AIACR) which was founded in Paris on this day in 1904.

Michael Schumacher won the United States GP at Indianapolis today in 2004 but he nearly retired voluntarily from the race midway through it after his brother Ralf had a big crash when one of his rear tyres deflated and threw his car into the wall at high speed. He was out of action for six races with his injuries.

JUNE 21

The fans at the Jarama circuit in Spain were in for a treat today in 1981 when they were able to enjoy one of the closest grands prix finishes ever. Ferrari's Gilles Villeneuve surged up through the order from seventh to lead by lap 14 with a trail of cars running closely behind him, led by Jacques Laffite. Villeneuve was faster on the straights but he was having to work hard to fight off challengers in the corners. For the last 18 laps the leading five cars were nose-to-tail. Villeneuve managed to hold them all off to win, with the first five cars all crossing the line within 1.24 seconds – the second closest race in the history of the sport at the time.

Like any good Brazilian Ayrton Senna was passionate about football. On this day in 1986 he qualified on pole for the Detroit GP and immediately left the circuit so he could watch Brazil take on France in the World Cup quarter-final, leaving a tape of his comments about the lap for the press. Brazil lost on penalties but Senna won the race the next day.

JUNE 22

When Lord Hesketh decided to start a racing team simply to have fun there was really only one driver that would be a perfect fit for it. James Hunt was signed up to drive for the squad that was famous for consuming more champagne than petrol during a race weekend, but today in 1975 the F1 establishment was forced to start taking them seriously when Hunt took his and Hesketh's maiden victory at the Dutch GP at Zandvoort. Although Hunt went on to become World Champion, this was Hesketh's only victory in the sport.

Today in 2005 BMW announced it was to pull the plug on the engine partnership with Williams and had decided to buy Peter Sauber's F1 team instead. The new BMW team took their first victory at Canada in June 2008.

JUNE 23

Another attempt to portray the world of racing hit the screens today in 1971 when Steve McQueen's film *Le Mans* was released in America. The film had very little dialogue but did have realistic racing scenes as the film crew took footage from the 1970 race. A keen racer himself, McQueen was almost ruined when the film was not a commercial success but his character Michael Delaney did come out with the memorable line: 'A lot of people go through life doing things badly. Racing's important to men who do it well. When you're racing, it... it's life. Anything that happens before or after... is just waiting.'

Today in 1991 F1 drivers Johnny Herbert, Bertrand Gachot and Volker Wiedler were celebrating after winning the Le Mans 24 Hours Race. They did it in a Japanese Mazda – it was the first time the prestigious race was won by a car made outside Western Europe.

JUNE 24

Nigel Mansell was pulling off one of the moves that earned him the nickname 'Il Leone' (The Lion) from the Tifosi today in 1990 at the Mexican Grand Prix. Alain Prost was leading in his Ferrari but behind him Gerhard Berger in the McLaren was desperately trying to stay in front of Mansell in the other Ferrari. On the last lap Mansell made his legendary move, taking Berger on the outside of the Peraltada corner. Murray Walker went up an octave describing the action: 'Mansell going round the outside! Incredible!' James Hunt was calmer as usual: 'Fantastically brave. Marvellous stuff by Mansell.'

Even racing drivers have to observe speed limits when driving on public roads but inevitably temptation proves too much. Today in 2003 Juan Pablo Montoya was banned from driving on French roads for four months after he was caught doing 126 mph in his BMW. He was also fined €1,200 but the ban did not stop his from racing in F1.

JUNE 25

To have any chance of success in motorsport in the 1930s you really had no option but to drive for one of the Nazi-funded German teams. British aristocrat Dick Seaman went to Europe and drove for the Mercedes Grand Prix team, famously winning the 1938 German Grand Prix with Hitler among the spectators. Today in 1939, while leading the Belgian Grand Prix at Spa, he crashed into a tree on lap 22 and died. He is reported to have told a Mercedes engineer on his death bed: 'I was going too fast for the conditions – it was entirely my own fault. I am sorry.'

Fernando Alonso continued his march to his second consecutive World Championship today in 2006 when he took victory in the Canadian Grand Prix. It was his fourth win in a row and his sixth of the season so far as the man from Spain looked unstoppable.

JUNE 26

We are going all the way back to 1906 today when the first ever grand prix race was held at Le Mans. The field of 32 cars set off at 90-second intervals to attempt 12 laps of the 64 mile course – all on public roads. After six laps the cars were taken into parc ferme and spent the night under guard before the race was resumed the next day. Ferenc Szisz, a Hungarian living in France, became the first man to win a grand prix race in his Renault, 32 minutes ahead of Felice Nazzaro's Fiat, with Albert Clément in third.

Today in 2002 Ferrari was fined $1m for breaking podium protocol at the Austrian GP when Michael Schumacher had pushed Rubens Barrichello onto the top step after the Brazilian had been ordered to gift the win to his teammate. No penalty was imposed for the use of team orders. Bernie Ecclestone said: 'There's team orders in bicycle racing and whatever. I don't think we should change it. It's a team event.'

JUNE 27

In 1926 motorsport's then governing body the AIACR established new regulations in time for the Grand Prix de l'ACF at Miramas in France. The new rules were not popular and only Bugatti turned up to contest the race. Just three drivers started: Bartolomeo Costantini, Jules Goux and Pierre de Vizcaya. Goux won with Constantini the only other finisher in what remained the most farcical grand prix ever until the 2005 United States GP when all the Michelin runners pulled out leaving just six cars to trail around pointlessly.

There was a much more exciting French GP today in 1999 when wet weather and clever team strategy decided the outcome. Rubens Barrichello had secured a surprise pole position for Stewart-Ford but Jordan's Heinz-Harald Frentzen took an even more surprising win when the team long-fuelled him while the safety car was out. It was the first of two victories for Jordan and HHF that season when he finished third in the championship.

JUNE 28

Jack Brabham started his own racing team in 1962 but it was not the Australian driver who took the team's first World Championship victory. That honour fell to American driver Dan Gurney who won the French Grand Prix at Rouen today in 1964. Gurney also took victory in the Mexican Grand Prix that year as the team began to establish itself as a force in the sport.

After being beaten to pole position for the 1998 French Grand Prix by one-lap specialist Mika Hakkinen, Michael Schumacher had his revenge in the race today when he took the victory. His teammate Eddie Irvine finished second giving Ferrari their first 1-2 finish since the Spanish Grand Prix in 1990 when Alain Prost led home Nigel Mansell.

JUNE 29

The earliest motor races were vast city-to-city endurance events that ran on public roads. When brothers Marcel, Louis and Fernand Renault began building cars they realised racing them would be a good way to promote their business. Today in 1902 Marcel Renault won the Paris-to-Vienna race in a car he had designed and built himself. Some three million people turned out to watch and cheer Renault to victory in the 615-mile, 15-hour long event. The following year he was killed in the Paris-to-Madrid race and soon road racing in Europe was banned.

On this day in 1980, 78 years later to the day since Renault's victory, the French team was in grand prix racing again, now with French drivers Rene Arnoux and Jean-Pierre Jabouille at the wheel for the French GP at Paul Ricard. Unfortunately they could not emulate the company founder and the race was won by Williams' Alan Jones. Arnoux had to settle for fifth place while Jabouille had gearbox problems and retired on lap one.

JUNE 30

The French Grand Prix has been held twice on this day in history, and both were flag-to-flag victories for British drivers, who both went on to win the title that season. The first was in 1963 when Jim Clark was in his pomp. After qualifying on pole, Clark drove away from the rest of the field in his Lotus and won by over a minute from Tony Maggs who was second for Cooper.

In 1996 Damon Hill was beaten to pole by Michael Schumacher but the German's Ferrari engine blew up on the parade lap. Hill then raced off in his Williams-Renault and won from his teammate Jacques Villeneuve in second. The two Benettons of Jean Alesi and Gerhard Berger finished behind them making it a 1-2-3-4 finish for Renault engines on French soil.

FORMULA ONE
On This Day

JULY

JULY 1

Some of the closest wheel-to-wheel racing ever in Formula One took place today in 1979 at the French GP at Dijon. Ferrari's Gilles Villeneuve and Frenchman René Arnoux in the Renault had a memorable battle for second place. Arnoux passed Villeneuve with three laps left but a daring wheel-locking move saw Villeneuve snatch the place back a lap later. They exchanged the position several times, each sliding off line and even banging wheels as they both refused to give an inch. In the end Villeneuve took the flag with his car just three tenths of a second ahead of Arnoux, who said: 'The duel with Gilles is something I'll never forget. You can only race like that with someone you trust completely, and you don't meet many like him. He beat me, yes and in France, but it didn't worry me. I knew I'd been beaten by the best driver in the world.'

Frenchman Jean-Pierre Jabouille actually won that day, also in a Renault – it was the first ever win in F1 for a turbocharged engine.

JULY 2

If you are only ever going to win one World Championship race, it might as well be your first. Giancarlo Baghetti was a young Italian driver who, on this day in 1961 won his very first World Championship event at the French GP at Reims in the famous sharknose Ferrari 156. The leading Ferrari drivers Wolfgang von Trips and Phil Hill both had problems in the race and on the last lap Baghetti was second to Dan Gurney's Porsche. Just 300 yards from the finish he pulled out of Gurney's slipstream and darted ahead, winning by just 0.1 of a second.

Formula One fans in Britain had an unfamiliar voice commentating on the French Grand Prix today in 2000 as Murray Walker missed the race because he had dislocated his hip. It was the first race he had missed since 1978 and James Allen deputised for him.

JULY 3

Today in 1966 Jack Brabham won the French Grand Prix at Reims. It was the first win for the former World Champion since the 1960 Portuguese Grand Prix but it was the first time ever that a driver had won a World Championship race in a car bearing his own name. Indeed the only other man to have achieved such a feat since is Brabham's one-time teammate Bruce McLaren.

The race was also the debut event for British driver Mike Parkes. He was an engineer and reserve driver at Ferrari and had been promoted to the race team after John Surtees walked out. He immediately proved his credentials by finishing second – one of the best ever debuts for an F1 driver.

JULY 4

Bernie Ecclestone may be the scariest man in the F1 paddock but out in the real world not everyone is so reverential towards him. Today in 1996 Bernie and his wife Slavica were mugged outside their luxury home in Chelsea Square, London. Unsurprisingly Bernie was not willing to watch the two muggers simply walk off with their loot and he challenged them and suffered a fractured cheekbone and had a trip to hospital for his troubles. The thieves got away with a Rolex watch and Mrs Ecclestone's diamond ring, rumoured to be worth more than $750,000.

One of the biggest modern-day mysteries is who is *Top Gear's* The Stig? Today in 2002 the tame racing driver was revealed as one-time F1 driver Perry McCarthy when he admitted to his secret identity in his book *Flat Out, Flat Broke*. The book also detailed his attempts to make it to F1 with no financial backing. The *Top Gear* bosses were not amused however and he was sacked from the programme for letting the secret out.

JULY 5

The early days of the Formula One World Championship were dominated by cars and drivers from Italy. It was not until 1953, the fourth year of the championship, that a British driver even won a race. It happened on this day at the French Grand Prix at Reims when Mike Hawthorn took the chequered flag for Ferrari. He and Juan Manuel Fangio in the Maserati fought a close battle for the win, the pair of them swapping the lead constantly during the final laps. Hawthorn won by just 40 yards from Fangio in the most exciting race since the World Championship began.

Alain Prost took his first F1 victory today in 1981 – just his second year in the sport. He won the French GP at Dijon for Renault. A maiden home win for a French driver in a French car was a fairytale start for Prost's winning ways and changed his mindset. 'Before, you thought you could do it,' he said. 'Now you know you can.'

JULY 6

It was truly the end of an era today in 1958 when perhaps the greatest driver of all time raced his last grand prix at Reims in France. Juan Manuel Fangio won five world titles between 1951 and 1957 and by 1958 he was still racing at the front at the age of 47. His last race was in a Maserati and winner Mike Hawthorn reportedly allowed the former champ to unlap himself before the end of the race.

The streets of London reverberated to the sound of screaming F1 engines today in 2004 when stars including Jenson Button, Nigel Mansell, Martin Brundle and Juan Pablo Montoya drove their cars down Regent Street in front of huge crowds. Simon Milton, leader of Westminster Council, said the council would love to put on a grand prix in London: 'Today is a taster but we are keen to enter into discussions to bring a grand prix to the centre of London.'

JULY 7

Jo Schlesser was a popular French racing driver in the 1960s who had most of his success in sports car racing. When Honda offered him their experimental, magnesium RA302 for the 1968 French GP at Rouen on this day, he couldn't refuse, despite the fact regular Honda tester John Surtees had declined to use the car saying it was not ready and potentially dangerous. On lap two he was proved right when Schlesser lost control, hit a bank and the car overturned and caught fire. He was unable to escape from the flames and was killed. He was the fourth driver to die that season after Jim Clark, Mike Spence and Lodovico Scarfiotti. When his friend Guy Ligier later became a constructor, he prefixed all his cars with 'JS' in memory of Schlesser.

Meanwhile the race continued and was won by Belgian Jacky Ickx in a Ferrari – his first victory in only his ninth grand prix.

JULY 8

The US GP at Dallas on this day in 1984 almost did not happen at all after the circuit was badly damaged by another race on the Saturday. Niki Lauda and Alain Prost tried to organise a boycott among the drivers but Bernie Ecclestone was having none of this Arthur Scargill action and the race went ahead after last minute repairs to the track. Larry Hagman, better known as JR Ewing from *Dallas*, waved the flag to start the race which Keke Rosberg won in his Williams-Honda.

Nigel Mansell had started from his first pole position and had led for half the race but the extreme heat took its toll on his tyres and he had to pit for new ones. On the last lap he ran out of fuel with just yards to go to the finish. Undeterred he climbed out and pushed his Lotus to the line to the delight of the crowd before collapsing at the side of his car. He was classified sixth.

JULY 9

The French Grand Prix at Paul Ricard today in 1989 was notable for one of those spectacular crashes that end up in compilation videos every Christmas. Prost and Senna started first and second in their all-conquering McLaren-Hondas but Senna managed to get the lead off the line. Behind them it was chaos as Mauricio Gugelmin locked his brakes in the middle of the pack and crashed into the back of Thierry Boutsen and Nigel Mansell. Gugelmin's March was flipped over dramatically while other drivers hit each other in the melee. The race was red flagged and restarted with all the drivers involved in the crash able to take to the spare car and compete. Alain Prost took victory ahead of Mansell and Riccardo Patrese.

Making his debut in the race was young French Sicilian driver Jean Alesi who had landed a drive with Tyrrell. He acquitted himself well and was even running in second place at one point before finishing a very impressive fourth in his home race.

JULY 10

After Ayrton Senna's tragic death it fell to Damon Hill to lead the Williams team and take the championship fight to Michael Schumacher. Today in 1994 Hill did just that when he won the British Grand Prix at Silverstone, something his father never achieved in 17 attempts. There was controversy after Schumacher overtook Hill on the parade lap and then ignored black flags indicating he should pit immediately. Eventually he did pit to give Hill a clear run to the finish but Schumi was later disqualified from his second place and banned for a further two races for ignoring the black flag.

Meanwhile Hill celebrated his win with a Union Jack flag given to him by a marshal on the slowing down lap, before he joined Eddie Jordan, Johnny Herbert and Eddie Irvine on the back of a lorry playing rock and roll with Jordan's band in the paddock.

JULY 11

Peter Rodriguez was a talented Mexican driver and the older brother of Riccardo, who was killed in practice for the Mexican Grand Prix in 1962. Peter considered retiring after the loss of his brother but he decided to continue racing and went on to become a top F1 driver, winning the South African GP in 1967 and the Belgian GP in 1970. Before he could really hit top form he too was killed on this day in 1971 in a sports car race at Norisring in Nuremberg.

There was another big accident on this day in 1999 when Michael Schumacher had a massive impact at Stowe corner at Silverstone in the opening lap of the British GP. His Ferrari failed to make the corner and ploughed straight into the tyre barrier. He broke his leg which put paid to his title chances with the Prancing Horse for another season.

JULY 12

After some success in motorbike racing and a slow start to his career on four wheels, by the early nineties Damon Hill was beginning to find his feet and managed to get an F1 drive with the moribund Brabham team. Today in 1992 at the British GP Hill started his first grand prix, having managed to qualify the uncompetitive Brabham for the first time. He finished 16th, four laps down on the leaders.

Martin Brundle summed up the British GP at Silverstone on this day in 1998 with the words, 'This is as bizarre as I've ever seen a finish of a grand prix.' Michael Schumacher had been leading in his Ferrari when he was given a stop and go penalty in the closing laps. It looked like victory was gone but Michael came in on the last lap to take his penalty, thereby crossing the finish line in the pits to win the race. Confusion reigned and Murray Walker could only say, 'I'm *pretty* sure that Michael Schumacher has won the British Grand Prix.'

JULY 13

Nigel Mansell was always good value on home soil and today in 1986 he won the British Grand Prix at Brands Hatch – the same track where he had taken his first victory the previous season. The race was very nearly over before it started for Mansell whose Williams broke down on the opening lap. Behind him a multiple car accident caused the race to be stopped so he was able to take to the spare car to win.

Today in 1999 as it became clear Michael Schumacher would be out for some time with his broken leg, Ferrari announced Finnish driver Mika Salo would drive in his absence. He had previously raced in F1 for Lotus, Tyrrell, Arrows and BAR and was highly rated by Ferrari boss Jean Todt. Salo said: 'I was lying in bed thinking, and I just could not stop smiling. All drivers dream of driving a Ferrari.'

JULY 14

Some people only watch motorsport for the crashes and they would not have been disappointed today in 1973 at the British GP at Silverstone when Jody Scheckter lost control and spun his car at Woodcote. His McLaren hit the pitwall and then bounced back into the middle of the track, just as the chasing pack arrived. With so many cars arriving and only so much track, a big shunt was inevitable and ten cars were caught up in the chaos as the race had to be restarted.

Nigel Mansell took the third British GP victory of his career today in 1991 having beaten his rival Ayrton Senna. After Mansell took the chequered flag, Senna's McLaren ground to a halt having run out of fuel while running in second. On his victory lap Mansell stopped at Senna's car and the Brazilian climbed aboard the Englishman's Williams for a lift back to the pits as the crowd cheered.

JULY 15

Ferrari utterly dominated the British Grand Prix at Aintree on this day in 1961. Phil Hill had qualified on pole for the Scuderia but on race day he was beaten to the flag by the German driver Wolfgang von Trips who led an impressive 1-2-3 for the Italian team, with Phil Hill and Ritchie Ginther following him home to make it an all-red podium. It was von Trips' second F1 win and sadly his last as he was killed at the Italian Grand Prix two months later.

Local hero Stirling Moss was having a good race until lap 44 when he pitted with brake problems. He did get going again but was eventually disqualified for receiving a push start. It was the last time he would race in F1 on home soil as injuries suffered in a crash in 1962 forced him to retire.

JULY 16

Stirling Moss took his first F1 victory at the British Grand Prix today in 1955, and became the first British driver to win the event since the series started in 1950. The race was held at Aintree near Liverpool and was a battle between Moss and reigning World Champion Juan Manuel Fangio, both of them driving Mercedes cars. The two swapped the lead throughout the race with Moss just emerging ahead of his rival when it counted at the chequered flag. He won by just two-tenths of a second and always maintained Fangio had let him win but the Argentine never admitted it.

Being Michael Schumacher's teammate often means you are something of an afterthought within the team but today in 1995 Johnny Herbert stole the limelight for a change when he won the British Grand Prix with Benetton – his first F1 win. A trademark Schumacher/Hill clash on the track had taken them both out and Herbert raced to the flag to cap a hugely popular debut win for one of the most popular drivers in the pitlane.

JULY 17

The British Grand Prix at Silverstone held on this day in 1954 was the first World Championship race entered by the Vanwall team. Started by British factory owner Tony Vandervell the team ran cars which had been built by Cooper. Peter Collins drove for them at Silverstone but the team suffered a fairly ignominious start when his engine failed on lap 16. The team went on to have success throughout the 1950s winning nine races and the first ever constructors' championship in 1958. Much of the team's success was down to Stirling Moss and a young designer named Colin Chapman who went on to found Lotus.

By 1971 it was another British team making the headlines when Tyrrell had the car to beat. On this day Jackie Stewart continued his march to the 1971 championship when he took a dominant victory in the British Grand Prix at Silverstone in the Tyrrell.

JULY 18

A big crowd at the British Grand Prix at Brands Hatch went home happy today in 1976 after seeing playboy Brit racer James Hunt take victory for McLaren. But all was not as it seemed. At the start of the race Ferrari teammates Niki Lauda and Clay Regazzoni touched and Regazzoni spun. Hunt hit Regazzoni and was launched into the air, damaging his car when he landed. The race was red-flagged and restarted and Hunt took to the spare car. He duly won, but Ferrari protested the result and in September Hunt was stripped of the win. Second-placed man Lauda inherited the win but it was not enough to stop Hunt taking the title by just one point from Lauda.

Hunt won three more races in 1977 but they would be McLaren's last for some four years. Today in 1981 the team ended their drought when John Watson won the British GP at Silverstone. It was the first win for the team since Ron Dennis took control.

JULY 19

The F1 circus was at Silverstone today in 1975 for the British Grand Prix. Before the race Graham Hill announced his retirement from driving after a stellar career including (a then record) 176 GPs and two World Championships. He is the only man in history to have won the triple crown of motorsport, defined as the Le Mans 24 Hours, the Indianapolis 500 and either the F1 World Championship or the Monaco GP. Hill has it under either definition.

The race itself was a chaotic affair that saw 16 runners crash out in the wet conditions, many at Club corner which created a pile up of F1 cars. No sooner had one driver jumped out of his car then another was sliding into it. The race was red-flagged and Emerson Fittipaldi declared the winner, with just six other cars still running. It was the double World Champion's last ever F1 win.

JULY 20

A sure sign that the British influence was growing in Formula One came today in 1957 at the British GP at Aintree. Stirling Moss had qualified on pole in his Vanwall and after an early tussle with Frenchman Jean Behra, Moss started to build his lead. Then, disaster, as his car broke down, forcing him to pit. Tony Brooks in the second Vanwall was called in and handed over his car to Moss. Behra was now leading but his clutch exploded on lap 69 and Moss was able to fight his way back up the order to take another popular home win. It was the first World Championship win for a British built car.

The British GP at Silverstone on this day in 2003 was interrupted by a track invader on lap 11. Former Catholic priest Cornelius 'Neil' Horan walked onto Hangar Straight wearing a kilt and brandishing a placard saying 'Read the Bible' and 'The Bible is Always Right'. Fortunately all the drivers managed to avoid him and he was later jailed for two months.

JULY 21

For decades no one thought anyone would ever match Fangio's achievement of winning five World Championship titles but today in 2002 it happened when Michael Schumacher won the French Grand Prix at Magny-Cours. Michael had equalled Fangio's 45-year-old record and he had done it in record time, taking just 11 races of the season to win the title. Emotional and close to tears afterwards Schumacher said: 'I have never been good at finding the right words at these moments. It has overcome me.' Ferrari chairman Luca di Montezemolo described Schumacher as 'the greatest driver to ever drive a Ferrari'.

While Ferrari and Schumacher were celebrating, the mood at the Arrows team was downcast. In serious financial difficulty, team boss Tom Walkinshaw was in negotiations to sell the team and the only running the cars did all weekend was one unsuccessful lap in qualifying which was enough to fulfill their contractual obligations. The team folded shortly afterwards.

JULY 22

When they were racing together in the early eighties many people thought Derek Warwick the more likely to achieve success than his British compatriot Nigel Mansell. A series of unfortunate career choices by Derek put paid to his World Championship ambitions and in the end he left F1 without a single race win. The closest he came was at the British GP at Brands Hatch on this day in 1984 when he finished second in a Renault to Niki Lauda's McLaren. The race was also notable because the Tyrrell team was banned for using lead balls in its water ballast. They appealed but to no avail and they were stripped of their points for the entire season.

Fernando Alonso won the European GP at the Nurburgring today in 2007 while listeners to BBC radio were able to enjoy the commentary of Murray Walker for the first time since he retired in 2001.

JULY 23

Until 2009 when he found himself in a race-winning Brawn GP car, Jenson Button has made something of a career of being in the wrong car at the wrong time. Today in 2002 he announced he would be joining BAR. 'BAR provided me with an excellent opportunity to progress and ultimately, I hope, to achieve my ambition to be World Champion,' he said.

Button's hopes of success were boosted today in 2004 when Honda extended their engine supply deal to BAR. The deal was a prelude to Honda buying the team outright in 2006.

JULY 24

Today in 1938 a young British aristocrat racer named Dick Seaman won the German Grand Prix at the Nurburgring driving a Mercedes-Benz and watched by Hitler. The young Brit, who was given a country estate for his 20th birthday, was no Nazi but simply wanted to win and so signed to drive for the Nazi-funded Mercedes team. He was the first Englishman to win a major grand prix since Major Henry Segrave in 1923. On the podium he gave a Nazi salute but said: 'I only wish it had been a British car.' A year later he was killed when pushing too hard at Spa. Hitler sent an enormous wreath and Mercedes still tends to his grave to this day.

Ageism is rife in sport and in 1966 there was much newspaper speculation that 40-year-old Jack Brabham was too old to be a serious challenger for the World Championship. Today at the Dutch GP at Zandvoort Jack limped to his car with the aid of a stick while sporting a false beard, much to the paddock's amusement. Needless to say he had the last laugh when he not only won the race, but also took the championship that season. He carried on racing until 1970.

JULY 25

The Renault team were celebrating today in 1982 when Rene Arnoux led home Alain Prost to secure the first ever 1-2 finish for the team – and at their home race, the French GP at Paul Ricard. Prost was livid with his teammate as he thought he should have allowed him to win to help his championship bid.

Heinz-Harald Frentzen was more than a match for Michael Schumacher in their early racing days in junior formulae but it never seemed to come together for him in Formula One. After a torrid spell with Williams Frentzen looked to have found his home with Jordan and even challenged for the championship with them in 1999. It was all over on this day in 2001 when HHF was suddenly sacked by Eddie Jordan over disagreements about the direction of the team.

JULY 26

Italian driver Antonio Ascari was killed on this day in 1925 while leading the French Grand Prix in an Alfa Romeo P2 at the Autodrome de Montlhéry near Paris. Ascari left behind a seven-year-old son, Alberto, who also went on to become a famous grand prix driver, and died in mysteriously similar circumstances to his father. Both died on the 26th day of the month, aged 36 and both drove car number 26. Both had won 13 grands prix and both died four days after surviving previous accidents. They both left a wife and two children.

When Mika Hakkinen stepped down from his race seat at McLaren for a sabbatical year in 2002 many speculated as to whether he would return to racing. Today in 2002 the Flying Finn announced he would not be returning to the cockpit. He said: 'I didn't want to hurt myself. I've been through so much in my career in F1, particularly in 1995, and I did achieve so much that I thought that it's not worth it any more to push your luck further.'

JULY 27

On this day in 1986 at the German GP at Hockenheim Alain Prost was coming over all Nigel Mansell when his McLaren ran out of fuel on the last lap on the finishing straight. Prost got out and tried to push his car over the line to great applause from the crowd. He didn't make it, but still earned a point for sixth place as the next car was over a lap down.

Gerhard Berger scored a popular victory in the German Grand Prix today in 1997. It was the Austrian's last F1 win, just as it was the last win for the Benetton team. Neatly, Berger's first win in 1986 had also been Benetton's first.

JULY 28

On this day in 1935 at the German Grand Prix at the Nurburgring the German-made Mercedes-Benz and Auto Union cars were supposed to dominate with their German drivers in front of the 300,000 fans and Nazi hierarchy that were present. Even Hitler himself had made it clear that a German victory was imperative. The Italian Tazio Nuvolari had not read the script, and in his less powerful Alfa Romeo he produced his finest grand prix performance to take a dramatic victory on the last lap. 'At first there was deathly silence,' *MotorSport* magazine reported, 'and then the innate sportsmanship of the Germans triumphed over their astonishment. Nuvolari was given a wonderful reception.'

The Nazi officials were not as pleased and did not even have the Italian national anthem on hand, so sure were they of a German victory. Nuvolari was able to produce his own record of the anthem which he always carried for luck.

JULY 29

The Nurburgring hosted a World Championship race for the first time today in 1951 for the German GP. Alberto Ascari took his first World Championship win for Ferrari.

It was a tragic day in grand prix racing today in 1973 at the Dutch GP at Zandvoort when young British driver Roger Williamson was killed in appalling circumstances during the race. A tyre problem caused him to crash and his car came to rest upside down and on fire at the side of the track. He was unable to get himself out and the marshals did nothing. Fellow driver David Purley stopped his car and ran to his friend's aid, grabbing a fire extinguisher from a marshal and trying to right the car by himself. His efforts were in vain and Williamson died in the car before a fire truck could reach the scene. Purely was awarded the George Medal but remained bitter that the marshals had not done more to help save his friend.

JULY 30

Track invaders at grands prix are just not as good as their streaker counterparts who interrupt football and cricket matches. In those cases everyone has a laugh and the offender is led off under a blanket before the game can resume. Invading a racetrack could result in fatalities. Today in 2000 at Hockenheim for the German GP a disgruntled Mercedes employee cut through the track fence and ran onto the track carrying a sheet with a message about the German car-maker. He even ran across the track before marshals eventually apprehended him.

The unexpected arrival of a man on the track turned the race upside down. Until that point Mika Hakkinen looked like leading home a McLaren 1-2 but after the safety car was deployed the order was mixed up allowing Rubens Barrichello to take his first F1 victory. He had started 18th on the grid. It was the first win for a Brazilian since Ayrton Senna's last win at Australia in 1993.

JULY 31

Dutch driver Jos Verstappen was always one of the most well supported by his many fans when he was in F1. Today in 1994 at the German GP Jos was caught up in a big fire while driving for Benetton. He came in for his first pitstop and the crew went to connect the fuel hose but fuel sprayed all over the car, including into his helmet as he had just opened his visor. A split second later the car was engulfed in flames and marshals and pit crews raced in to put the fire out. Jos 'the Boss' and some of the mechanics were treated for minor burns.

On this day in 2007 triple World Champion Nelson Piquet was ordered to attend a driving awareness school after losing his licence for repeated speeding and parking offences. His wife Viviane was also ordered to attend the course. 'We're going to make good use of this course and learn something,' he said graciously.

FORMULA ONE
On This Day

AUGUST

AUGUST 1

Jim Clark wrapped up his second World Championship today in 1965 when he won the German Grand Prix at the Nurburgring in dominant fashion for Lotus. It was his sixth victory out of seven races so far in a season when few drivers could touch him.

Today in 1976 at the German GP at the Nurburgring Niki Lauda had a huge accident when his Ferrari went off the track, burst into flames and then bounced back into the middle of the track where it was hit by two other cars. Drivers Guy Edwards, Harald Ertl, Brett Lunger and Arturo Merzario managed to pull Lauda out of his car but he suffered serious burns and other injuries and was even read the last rites by a priest. Amazingly he recovered and was back behind the wheel just six weeks later.

AUGUST 2

Since the start of the World Championship in 1950 the German Grand Prix has always been run at the Nurburgring or at Hockenheim, with one exception. Today in 1959 the race was held at the curious AVUS circuit in Berlin. The track is really just two long stretches of motorway with a hairpin at each end and is now part of a public road. The race was split into two heats amid concerns that tyres wouldn't last. British driver Tony Brooks won for Ferrari with Americans Dan Gurney and Phil Hill making it an all Ferrari podium.

The 1970 German GP held on this day was switched to Hockenheim at the last minute after the drivers refused to race at the Nurburgring until safety was improved. Austrian Jochen Rindt won to take him 20 points clear in the championship but it was his last ever win as he was killed later in the season at the Italian GP to become F1's only posthumous World Champion.

AUGUST 3

English driver Peter Collins was a favourite of Enzo Ferrari after he selflessly gave up his car for Fangio at the Italian GP in 1956 when Collins himself still had a chance of becoming champion. Today in 1958 Collins was pushing hard in the German Grand Prix at the Nurburgring when he went wide and one of his wheels got caught in a ditch. His Ferrari somersaulted across the track and Collins was thrown into a tree. He died later that day from severe head injuries.

At the Hungarian Grand Prix on this day in 2008 another Ferrari driver hit trouble, albeit much less serious. Felipe Massa looked to have the race sewn up when just three laps from the end his engine blew up and he coasted to a halt on the main straight. 'Racing can be a cruel sport,' he said. His misfortune handed a maiden victory to McLaren's latest Flying Finn, Heikki Kovalainen.

AUGUST 4

It is easy to look at Fangio simply in terms of statistics; he won 24 of his 51 grands prix, took 27 pole positions and was World Champion five times. On this day in 1957 he showed just how he racked up such impressive stats when he drove the race of his life to win the German GP at the Nurburgring. A bad pitstop put him more than a minute adrift of Hawthorn in the lead but he then set about reeling the Englishman in with a series of stunning laps. His best was some six seconds better than his own lap record and eight seconds faster than his pole time. It was his last victory and it clinched him his fifth World Championship. He said: 'I'd never driven like that before, and I knew I never would again.'

Jackie Stewart also produced perhaps his greatest ever drive at the Nurburgring today in 1968. In soaking conditions he totally outclassed everyone else to finish four minutes ahead of Graham Hill in second.

AUGUST 5

Michael Schumacher took time out of his World Championship winning schedule today in 1995 when he got married to Corinna Betsch. The new Mrs Schumi obviously has something of a penchant for German racing drivers, having previously been Heinz-Harald Frentzen's girlfriend before she started going out with Michael.

On this day in 2004 Williams announced they had re-signed Jenson Button for the 2005 and '06 seasons. The team he was with at the time, BAR-Honda, claimed he was contracted to them and the case went to Formula One's Contract Recognition Board which ruled in BAR's favour. A year later he was bizarrely caught up in the opposite position: having signed a deal to drive for Williams for 2006 he decided he wanted to stay at BAR and after a lengthy dispute he had to pay out a reported £20m to Williams to release him from the deal.

AUGUST 6

Today in 2006 was a better day for Button when he finally took his first F1 victory for Honda in the Hungarian Grand Prix at the Hungaroring. He had started way down the grid in 14th but helped by the wet conditions and a safety car appearance, Jense carved his way through the field to win for the first time in 113 attempts. He said: 'What a day – it's been amazing. Coming through from 14th to win the race was brilliant. I could not have done it a better way.'

Robert Kubica began his F1 career in the same race, making his debut for the BMW Sauber team after regular driver Jacques Villeneuve sat the race out after an accident in the previous race. The young Polish driver impressed by qualifying ninth and finishing seventh before he was disqualified after his car was found to be underweight. Nonetheless he kept his seat and was soon signed up as a full-time driver for 2007.

AUGUST 7

Because there was only a small entry of Formula One cars at the 1966 German Grand Prix, the organisers decided to let the F2 cars run at the same time. In the race Jim Clark made a rare mistake and crashed out leaving Jack Brabham to pick up his fourth consecutive win. Jacky Ickx and Englishman John Taylor were among the F2 runners and the two collided on the opening lap. Both cars spun off and Taylor's burst into flames. The driver from Leicester suffered serious burns and died a month later from his injuries.

The McLaren-Honda team continued their extraordinary season of dominance today in 1988 at the Hungarian Grand Prix at the Hungaroring. Ayrton Senna led Alain Prost home for yet another 1-2 finish – one of ten for McLaren in a season when they only lost one race.

AUGUST 8

Brazil and Argentina have a rich history of producing top F1 stars, but neighbouring Chile do not have such a good pedigree. Eliseo Salazar is the only Chilean to have competed in the sport and he is most famous for being attacked by three-time World Champion Nelson Piquet during the German GP at Hockenheim on this day in 1982. Piquet was leading the race and coming up to lap backmarker Salazar who failed to slow down and crashed into Piquet, taking them both out of the race. The Brazilian was furious and got out of the car and attacked Salazar, pushing him and trying to kick him as amazed spectators looked on. Murray Walker suddenly found himself commentating on a fight instead of a motor race, 'And take that!' he cried as Piquet went for hapless Chilean.

After Eddie Jordan sacked Heinz-Harald Frentzen halfway through the 2001 season the Irishman moved quickly to replace him and immediately signed up his old friend Jean Alesi, on this day.

AUGUST 9

Lady luck is a fickle mistress and Nigel Mansell often seemed to be on her bad side. Nige was leading the Hungarian Grand Prix today in 1987 ahead of his bitter rival and Williams teammate Nelson Piquet, but five laps before the end Mansell lost a right rear wheel nut and was forced to retire, handing victory to Piquet.

Lewis Hamilton and Fernando Alonso were teammates who, like Mansell and Piquet, rarely saw eye to eye. During qualifying for the 2007 Hungarian GP Alonso held up Hamilton in the pit box, scuppering the Englishman's chance of taking pole. Hamilton was furious and the press reported that he had sworn at Ron Dennis over the radio but a McLaren statement issued on this day denied it: 'The team have investigated this claim and reviewed the radio transmissions and we can categorically confirm that Lewis did not use the "F" word at any time during any conversation with the team.'

AUGUST 10

Today in 1986 Formula One went behind the Iron Curtain for the first time when the first Hungarian Grand Prix was held at the Hungaroring outside Budapest. Some 200,000 spectators turned up to watch a good battle between Brazilians Nelson Piquet and Ayrton Senna, which Piquet won.

Damon Hill so nearly pulled off the most impressive and surprising victory of his grand prix career on this day in 1997. He had put his Arrows A18 third on the grid for the Hungarian GP. During the race he achieved a measure of personal redemption when he overtook Michael Schumacher and thereafter it looked like he would race to a famous victory. With just three laps to go, disaster: the Arrows had a hydraulic failure and Hill saw his 35-second lead over Jacques Villeneuve vanish. The Canadian passed Hill on the last lap and the Englishman had to settle for a heartbreaking second place. He said: 'I was beginning to think I could win and when you do that something always goes wrong.'

AUGUST 11

Tazio Nuvolari was the ultimate pre-war driver who won every major race going. 'Il Maestro' was described by Ferdinand Porsche as: 'The greatest driver of the past, the present, and the future.' Famed for his grit and determination as much as his speed, he once had his Maserati specially adapted so he could drive in a race with his leg still in plaster after he had broken it in a crash a month earlier. He died on this day in 1953 from a stroke aged 60. Alberto Ascari, Luigi Villoresi and Juan Fangio pushed his coffin on a car chassis on the mile-long funeral procession as all of Italy mourned.

Today in 1996 Jacques Villeneuve won the Hungarian Grand Prix at the Hungaroring – his third victory of his maiden Formula One campaign. He led home Damon Hill in a Williams 1-2 which wrapped up the constructors' championship for Sir Frank Williams' team for the eighth time – equaling Ferrari's record. The result also meant Villeneuve and Hill were now the only drivers who could win the drivers' title – a contest that would go down to the final race in Japan when the Englishman triumphed.

AUGUST 12

Alan Jones won the Austrian GP at the Osterreichring today in 1979 – it was the third of four consecutive wins for the Williams team but it was not enough in the end and Ferrari and Jody Scheckter won both championships that season.

Belgian driver Thierry Boutsen never really challenged for the World Championship but he won three races while he was with the Williams team. His third and last victory was arguably his finest when today in 1990 he won the Hungarian Grand Prix. He was under intense pressure throughout the race from his friend Ayrton Senna in the McLaren-Honda but he stood firm and made no mistakes to cross the line just inches ahead of Senna.

AUGUST 13

Along with Stirling Moss, 'Super Swede' Ronnie Peterson is regarded as one of the best drivers never to have won the World Championship. He took ten victories in an eight-year F1 career; the last was at the Austrian GP today in 1978 when he won for Lotus. He was killed a month later in a crash at the Italian Grand Prix at Monza.

Japanese driver Taki Inoue made a much smaller impact on F1. He spent a little over one season in the sport and is best remembered for a couple of bizarre accidents he was involved with. The first was at Monaco in 1995 when his Footwork car was being towed back to the pits during practice when the course car crashed into him. The second was at the Hungarian GP today in 1995 when his car had broken down. When he got out of his car the hapless Inoue ran right into the path of a marshal's car which knocked him down and injured his leg.

AUGUST 14

The Ferrari name is more than a racing team and a carmaker. The Prancing Horse is by far the most emotive and successful racing team in the history of Formula One and it was all started by Enzo Ferrari who founded the team in 1947. The Old Man remained in charge of the team until he died, aged 90, on this day in 1988.

In all the years the Ferrari team has been running many other outfits have come and gone from Formula One. One of those teams now long forgotten is Shadow. The team debuted in 1973 and had some talented drivers in their cars including Peter Revson, Jean-Pierre Jarier and Tom Pryce. The team scored their only F1 victory today in 1977 at the Austrian GP with Alan Jones – it was the Australian's first win.

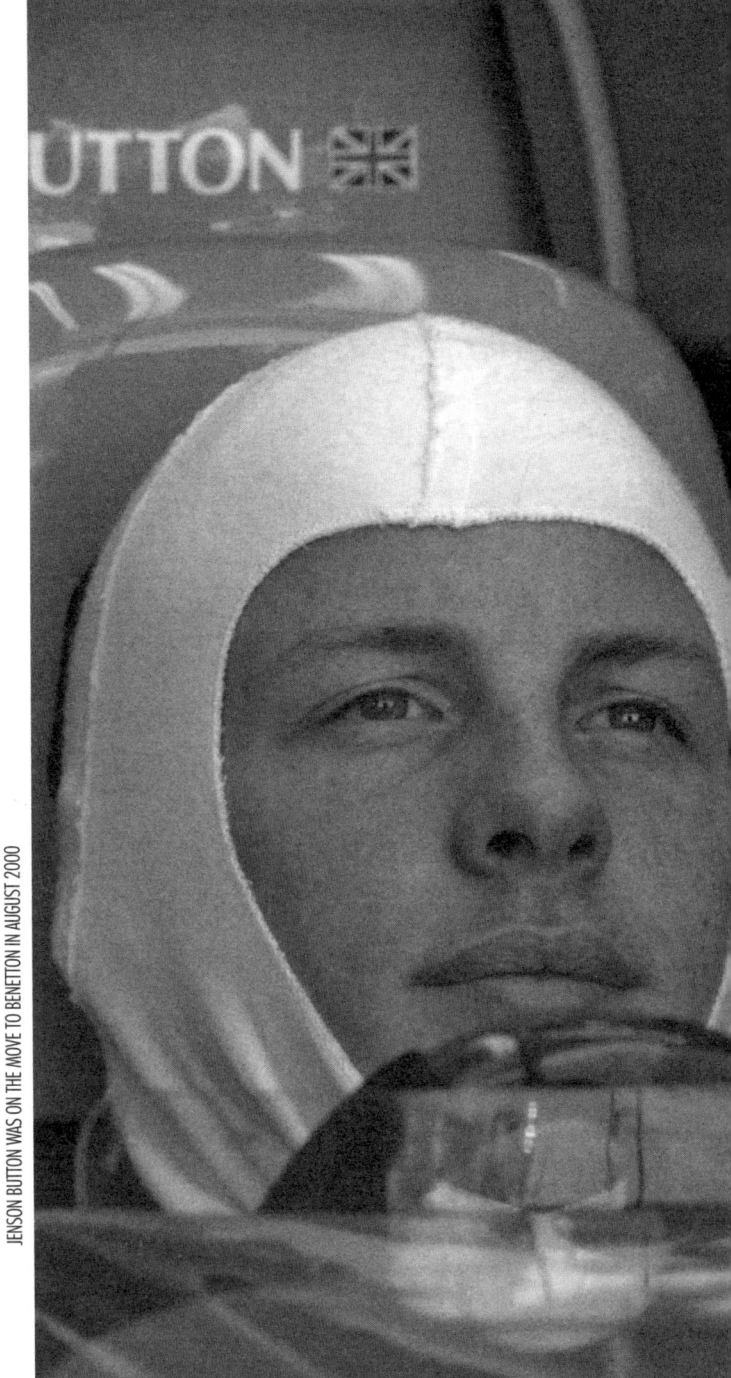

AUGUST 15

Swiss racer Jo Siffert won the Austrian Grand Prix today in 1971 at the Österreichring for BRM. It was his second F1 victory after the 1968 British Grand Prix but would prove to be his last as he was killed in a non-championship race at Brands Hatch later in the year.

Roger Penske is a highly successful team owner in the United States and his eponymous team has won Indy Car and NASCAR championships galore since it was started in the 1960s. In the 1970s Penske started an F1 team and hired John Watson to drive. Today in 1976 Watson won the Austrian Grand Prix – it was his first victory and the first and only for the Penske team. Racing lore has it that Watson was forced to shave off his beard after the victory having promised Roger Penske he would if the team won a race.

AUGUST 16

Nigel Mansell might have been forgiven for thinking he was destined to be forever the bridesmaid, never the World Champion, as he finished runner-up in 1986, 1987 and 1991. Today in 1992 he finally achieved his dream when he became World Champion after finishing second in the Hungarian Grand Prix in a Williams. It was a dominant season for the Englishman and he won nine out of 16 races. By clinching the title at Hungary, the 11th race of the season, he set a new record for winning the title in the least number of grands prix since the 16-race season was adopted.

As Mansell was flourishing with Williams, another famous name from F1 was fading away. The Brabham team was struggling for money and was rife with political infighting. The Hungarian race was the last grand prix the team entered before it folded. Damon Hill trundled home four laps down on the leaders to bring a sad end to the once-dominant team.

AUGUST 17

The Dutch are passionate about motor racing as the many fans of Jos Verstappen so colourfully illustrated when he was in Formula One. On this day in 1952 Holland hosted its first ever World Championship event, the Dutch GP at Zandvoort. To add to the occasion local hero and former Second World War flying ace Jan Flinterman made his F1 debut in the race to become the first Dutchman to compete in the sport. He drove a Maserati and managed to finish ninth, but it was his one and only grand prix and he went back to flying afterwards.

Today in 2000 Jenson Button's future was in the news again when it was announced he would be loaned by Frank Williams to the Benetton team for two seasons. Button said: 'I will always be eternally grateful to Frank Williams and Patrick Head at Williams for giving me my great opportunity in Formula One. I have some unfinished business at Williams.'

AUGUST 18

Stirling Moss won the Pescara Grand Prix in Italy on this day in 1957. The Pescara circuit is remembered as the longest track to ever stage a World Championship grand prix. At 16 miles long Moss's pole position lap was 9m 44.6s and the race only lasted 18 laps.

Wild man Italian driver Andrea de Cesaris was living up to his nickname 'Andrea de Crasheris' at the Austrian GP today in 1985 when he had yet another spectacular accident; his Ligier went off the track and was pitched into a series of dramatic rolls. He walked away unscathed but on arrival back at the pits he was promptly sacked by Guy Ligier. The French team owner was getting fed up with having to pay for costly repairs to his cars and reportedly said, 'I can no longer afford the services of this young man.'

AUGUST 19

When Roger Penske decided to compete in Formula One, he lured his old friend Mark Donohue out of retirement to drive for his team. It would be a fatal move as in practice for the 1975 Austrian GP Donohue crashed. He was seemingly unhurt but later slipped into a coma and died on this day.

It was a record breaking race for both Michael Schumacher and Ferrari at the Hungaroring today in 2001 when Schumi led home Rubens Barrichello in a Ferrari 1-2. The win wrapped up Michael's fourth drivers' title, equalling Alain Prost, and he also equalled the Frenchman's record of 51 grand prix victories. The 1-2 finish meant Ferrari also won the constructors' title for a record 11th time. 'It has been a beautiful weekend,' Schumacher said. 'We did everything we could have done. I came here with not such a good feeling, for whatever reason but we got pole position, we got the victory, I obviously equalled the 51 wins with Alain. And I got my fourth championship so, it's a bit too much for me right now to take it all in.'

AUGUST 20

The Renault team announced today in 2003 that its driver line-up of Jarno Trulli and Fernando Alonso would remain unchanged for the following season. 'This driver line-up provides us with a perfect balance,' team boss Flavio Briatore said. 'Next year will be Jarno's eighth season in Formula One, and everybody knows he is an extremely fast, competitive racing driver. Fernando has more than justified the faith we showed in him last year, and is maturing with the team as he acquires experience at the highest level.'

By 2005 Trulli had moved to Toyota but Alonso was fighting for his first World Championship title. Today in 2005 Alonso qualified third on the grid for the Turkish GP, with Trulli in fifth. No one could touch Kimi Raikkonen though who stormed to pole and then the win.

AUGUST 21

In 1988 Johnny Herbert was the coming man of motorsport and after impressive performances in the Formula Ford, British F3 and F3000 series his name was being touted as a future F1 star, and he had already set some fast times testing Benetton and Lotus F1 cars. On this day in 1988 at an F3000 race at Brands Hatch Herbert's future was thrown into doubt when he was caught up in a huge accident triggered by Swiss driver Gregor Foitek. Johnny's legs took the brunt of the massive impact and he was lucky not to lose one of his feet. He astounded doctors with his determination to recover and despite the fact he could barely walk he returned to the cockpit in early 1989, finishing a heroic fourth on his F1 debut for Benetton in Brazil.

Bernie Ecclestone continued his expansion of Formula One into new markets today in 2005 when the first ever Turkish Grand Prix was held in Istanbul. The new circuit immediately proved a hit with the F1 circus and Kimi Raikkonen took victory for McLaren.

AUGUST 22

Juan Manuel Fangio won the Swiss Grand Prix at Bermgarten today in 1954 for Mercedes-Benz. He was challenged early on by Stirling Moss, Mike Hawthorn and Froilan Gonzalez but soon took complete control and won by nearly a minute having overtaken every car up to Gonzalez in second. The victory was Fangio's fifth of the season and meant he won his second World Championship with two races to spare.

The race was the last ever grand prix held in Switzerland as the government banned motorsport in 1955 after the Le Mans disaster in which 80 spectators were killed. There was a Swiss Grand Prix in 1982 but the race was actually held at Dijon in France.

AUGUST 23

Today in 1964 was a day of firsts. It was the first time Austria hosted a World Championship grand prix which was won by Italian Lorenzo Bandini for Ferrari – his first and only F1 win. It was also the first grand prix for Jochen Rindt who became the first Austrian to race in F1.

Didier Pironi was at the centre of one of the biggest disputes in Formula One history when he took a last-gasp win away from Ferrari teammate Gilles Villeneuve at the 1982 San Marino GP. Villeneuve vowed never to speak Pironi ever again and kept his vow when he was killed just two weeks later. Today in 1987 Pironi himself suffered an untimely end when he was killed racing a powerboat in the Solent. The boat flipped and his two crew members, journalist Bernard Giroux and Jean-Claude Guenard, were also killed. Just weeks later Pironi's girlfriend gave birth to twins. She named them Gilles and Didier.

AUGUST 24

There is a temptation to romanticise the gentlemanly conduct of yesteryear's drivers but in the case of Sir Stirling Moss it is entirely justified. Moss was never World Champion and the closest he came was in 1958. At the Portuguese GP on this day that year Moss won ahead of Mike Hawthorn. The stewards threatened to disqualify Hawthorn for the small offence of restarting in the wrong direction after a spin. Moss leapt to his rival's defence and Hawthorn was allowed to keep his points. He went on to beat Moss in the title race by just one point.

The 2003 season saw eight different winners in the 16 races and today in that year Fernando Alonso became the latest man to take the top spot on the podium when he took his first grand prix victory. The Spaniard became the youngest ever GP winner at 22 years and 26 days and it was Renault's first win as a constructor since they returned to the sport in 2000.

AUGUST 25

In 1991 Bertrand Gachot was driving in F1 for the new Jordan team but he was jailed for assaulting a London cabbie the year before. No one could have foreseen the ramifications this would have for F1. Eddie Jordan turned to young German driver Michael Schumacher to fill the seat for the Belgian GP at Spa on this day, and he astounded the paddock by qualifying the slow car in seventh position. A clutch problem ruined his race chances but he had already announced his arrival.

As founder and principal of the Tyrrell team, Ken Tyrrell was the senior member of the partnership with his driver Jackie Stewart that delivered three World Championships in the sixties and seventies. On this day in 2001 'Uncle Ken' passed away at his home in Surrey. Stewart led the tributes and said: 'Ken was the most important person in my life outside my family. Without Ken Tyrrell, I would not be where I am today.'

AUGUST 26

Sports fans crave a bit of colour in their heroes and Gilles Villeneuve delivered that in spades. At the Dutch GP at Zandvoort on this day in 1979 the Canadian suffered a rear puncture causing him to spin. Rather than admit defeat he restarted his Ferrari and drove back to the pits – almost an entire lap on three wheels, his left rear wheel dragging along behind him, pulling wheelies and waving to the crowd as he went.

Also on this day in 1996 one of the longest team/sponsor associations was over when Marlboro announced its sponsorship deal with McLaren would not be renewed at the end of the season. Walter Thoma, president of Philip Morris EEC region said, 'During our 23 years of sponsorship, the Marlboro McLaren team has had unprecedented success, winning nine Drivers' World Championships, seven World Constructors' Championships and 96 grands prix. We are very proud of that record.'

AUGUST 27

Murray Walker was horrified when he was told he was being joined in the commentary box by James Hunt in 1980, but the pair soon forged a good working relationship, when Hunt turned up that is. Today in 1989 the former World Champion was nowhere to be found when the Belgian Grand Prix at Spa started so Muzza had to go it alone, although he was joined during the race by Johnny Herbert and Martin Brundle who had both retired from the race.

Michael Schumacher has said that Mika Hakkinen was his most worthy adversary and today in 2000 at Spa the two had one of their most memorable duels. In the closing stages Schumacher was leading but Hakkinen was looking to overtake. Soon both men were coming up to lap Ricardo Zonta on the Kemmel Straight. Schumi went left, but Hakkinen darted right and took them both. It was the Finn's best ever overtaking manoeuvre and won him the race.

AUGUST 28

When the BAR team entered F1 in 1999 they made wild predictions about winning their very first race, to howls of derision from more seasoned observers. In the end they didn't score a single point all season and probably the team's most noteworthy race was the Belgian GP at Spa. Jacques Villeneuve always attempted Eau Rouge flat out and today in qualifying he destroyed his car on the famous corner. His teammate, rookie Ricardo Zonta, also attempted to take the corner flat out, and had an even bigger crash. Neither driver was hurt but the mechanics had a long night rebuilding the cars in time for the race.

After Alex Zanardi lost both his legs after an accident in 2001 few people thought he would ever return to racing but today in 2005 the Italian won his first race since the crash, triumphing in the second race at a World Touring Car Championship event in Germany in a BMW.

AUGUST 29

The original Flying Finn was Keke Rosberg and he won the 1982 World Championship with Williams despite only winning one race all season. He took that victory on this day at the so-called Swiss Grand Prix, although it was held at Dijon in France, with motor racing still banned in Switzerland after the 1955 Le Mans disaster. Rosberg started eighth on the grid but overtook Alain Prost in the Renault late on in the race to take his first and all-important F1 victory.

At the Belgian Grand Prix at Spa today in 2004 Kimi Raikkonen took McLaren's first victory of the season but it was not enough to prevent Michael Schumacher from taking his seventh drivers' title. The Red Baron finished second to wrap up his last, and his easiest championship in a season that he and Ferrari dominated.

AUGUST 30

The start of any grand prix is always the most dangerous moment when the whole grid is so tightly bunched up. On this day in 1998 at the Belgian Grand Prix at Spa David Coulthard triggered a massive accident in the opening stages in which 13 cars were involved. Despite spectacular carnage no one was hurt and after the race was restarted rainmeister Michael Schumacher looked to have the win sewn up as he raced away from the rest of the field until he crashed into the back of David Coulthard while trying to lap him. A furious Schumacher had to be restrained by Ferrari staff after he marched into the McLaren garage screaming at Coulthard, even claiming the Scot had tried to kill him.

Meanwhile the racing continued and Damon Hill took the win, the first ever for the Jordan team, and Damon's first since 1996. To further sweeten the day for Eddie Jordan, Ralf Schumacher came second to make it a Jordan 1-2, although the German was upset he hadn't been given the chance to race Hill for the win in the closing stages.

AUGUST 31

Australian driver Alan Jones became the first man to win the World Championship with the Williams team in 1980. Today in that year, the Dutch Grand Prix at Zandvoort was the only grand prix that Jones finished not in a podium position. He had a big crash in practice but still qualified fourth. He then made a good start to take the lead but on the second lap he drove over a kerb and damaged one of the skirts on his car. He was forced to pit for repairs and eventually struggled to the flag in 11th place, three laps down on winner Nelson Piquet.

Another Antipodean was hoping to be setting a new record at the same race. Tyrrell's New Zealand test driver Mike Thackwell was given the chance to become the youngest ever entrant in a Formula One race at 19 years and 154 days. He got his chance when Arrows' Jochen Mass was too injured to drive and the Tyrrell team agreed to loan Thackwell to them. Sadly he was unable to qualify so missed the chance.

FORMULA ONE
On This Day

SEPTEMBER

SEPTEMBER 1

Although the Formula One World Championship began in 1950, grand prix racing had been developing at a pace after racing resumed after the war. The consensus among racing fans is that the first race run to F1 rules was held on the streets of Turin on this day in 1946. Achille Varzi won the Valentino Grand Prix in his factory Alfa Romeo although even in those days, long before Michael Schumacher was on the scene, team orders were controversial and fans at the race felt Jean-Pierre Wimille would have won in the other Alfa, had he been allowed to.

Steffan Bellof is remembered by F1 fans as the young driver who was catching both Alain Prost and Ayrton Senna in the rain-soaked 1984 Monaco GP when it was red-flagged. Today in 1985 the German driver was killed racing a Porsche 956 in a sports car race at Spa. He crashed at the fearsome Eau Rouge corner and was dead within an hour.

SEPTEMBER 2

The first British F1 champion was Mike Hawthorn but it could well have been Hawthorn's close friend Peter Collins were it not for a selfless act by the Englishman on this day in 1956. It was the Italian Grand Prix at Monza, the last race of the season, and any one of Stirling Moss, Collins or his teammate Fangio could have won the title. Halfway through the race Fangio dropped out with a broken steering arm but with just 15 laps to go, Collins pitted and despite being in a position to take the championship himself, he handed his car over to Fangio who went on to finish second and take his fourth drivers' title.

Today in 2001 Michael Schumacher broke Alain Prost's record of race wins to become the most successful race winner in the history of Formula One. Victory at the Belgian GP took him to 52 wins, not out.

SEPTEMBER 3

Yugoslavia hosted its one and only grand prix on this day in 1939. The Belgrade City race took place on the streets of the city and was won by Italian superstar Tazio Nuvolari for Auto Union ahead of a string of German drivers backed by the Third Reich. The race was the last grand prix event before the Second World War halted all racing activity.

Once hostilities were over and racing started up again it was decided to form a proper World Championship which started in 1950. On this day that year Italian driver Giuseppe Farina won the Italian Grand Prix at Monza. It was the final round of the seven-race season and victory made Farina the first ever F1 World Champion as he finished three points ahead of his rival Juan Manuel Fangio.

SEPTEMBER 4

The Italian Grand Prix at Monza today in 2005, won by McLaren's Juan Pablo Montoya, was only the second time in F1 history that all the cars that started the race were still running at the end. The other occasion was the Dutch Grand Prix in 1961.

One of those finishers was Italian Giancarlo Fisichella who finished third behind Montoya in first and Renault teammate Fernando Alonso in second. Fisi dedicated his podium to former F1 driver and fellow Italian Michele Alboreto who had been killed testing an Audi car in April 2001. Fisi said: 'I know Alboreto was the last Italian on the podium at Monza before me. I was lucky enough to race together with him in touring cars, and he was a great person, really special. I want to dedicate the result to his memory.'

SEPTEMBER 5

The 1970 grand prix season was turning out to be one of the most deadly after both Bruce McLaren and Piers Courage had been killed at the wheel of F1 cars. Things got even worse on this day that year when, in practice for the Italian GP at Monza, championship leader Jochen Rindt was killed after crashing heavily in his Lotus at the fateful Parabolica corner. He was leading the title race when he was killed and went on to be the only posthumous World Champion in the history of the sport.

British driver Peter Gethin won just one grand prix in his F1 career, but it was a belter of a race. The 1971 Italian GP at Monza was a thrilling battle in which eight different drivers held the lead at various points. Coming into the last lap the crowd was on its feet as there was nothing to choose between the first five runners. Gethin made his move at the Parabolica and just managed to finish ahead of Ronnie Peterson by just 0.01 seconds. The first five cars were covered by just 0.61 seconds and it was the closest finish in F1 history at the time.

SEPTEMBER 6

Englishman John Surtees delighted the Tifosi today in 1964 with victory in the Italian Grand Prix at Monza at the wheel of a Ferrari. The victory helped him to win the World Championship that season making him the only man in history to have won World Championships on two as well as four wheels. The race was also the last for French driver Maurice Trintignant who retired at the age of 47. He was the first Frenchman to win a World Championship race and won the prized Monaco GP twice.

Today in 1970 Clay Regazzoni took his first F1 victory in the Italian Grand Prix at Monza but there was little celebrating in the paddock as Lotus driver Jochen Rindt had been killed in practice the day before.

SEPTEMBER 7

There is nothing quite as special for a racing driver as winning the Italian Grand Prix in a Ferrari but Niki Lauda went one better today in 1975 when his third place in the race meant he and Ferrari won both championships on home soil.

After an exciting Belgian Grand Prix at Spa, Lewis Hamilton fans were celebrating after another victory for the young British charger, with some trademark racey overtaking moves thrown in for good measure. But alas for them and Hamilton the celebrations proved short lived as the stewards took a dim view of his moves on Raikkonen as they adjudged he had gained an advantage from missing the chicane, despite Lewis backing off to hand the position back to Kimi after the corner. Despite collecting the winner's medal on the podium he was later stripped of the win and dropped to third after getting a 25-second penalty.

SEPTEMBER 8

While many race fans support their favourite drivers through thick and thin, for Italian F1 fans it is all about Ferrari and their favourite driver is whoever is doing the business at the wheel of the blood-red cars. In 1996 Michael Schumacher joined Ferrari and on this day he achieved the ultimate for a Prancing Horse driver when he took victory at Monza. He said: 'I have never seen such emotion. It's crazy. It is only possible in Italy. It's fantastic. You get goose bumps everywhere. They have waited a long time for this and they deserve it.'

German manufacturers have a strong heritage in grand prix racing going all the way back to the Auto Union and Mercedes cars in the very early days of the sport. Today in 1997 another German marque announced it was returning to the sport it left in 1986. BMW revealed plans to supply engines to Williams from 2000 for five years.

SEPTEMBER 9

Lewis Hamilton was the beneficiary of a bit of stewarding interference when he was racing in GP2 today in 2006. Giorgio Pantano had set the fastest lap but was not given the customary one point for it because he had set it under yellow flags. The point went to Hamilton instead who had set the second fastest time and with it he won the GP2 championship in his last year in the series.

Eddie Jordan sold his eponymous F1 team in 2005 to the Russian-Canadian Alex Shnaider and today in 2006 the team was sold on again to the Dutch sports car maker Spyker. The team was sold on yet again in 2007 when it became Force India.

SEPTEMBER 10

The penultimate race of the season at Monza on this day in 1961 saw the Ferrari drivers Wolfgang von Trips and Phil Hill pitched against each other for the drivers' title, but the racing was overshadowed by a shocking accident at the start when Jim Clark and von Trips collided as they approached Parabolica. Clark was unhurt but von Trips' car hit a spectator fence and was thrown into a roll, killing von Trips and 14 spectators. Phil Hill went on to win and become the first American F1 champion.

Clark was unhurt that day and lined up on pole at Monza again on this day in 1967 when he produced one of his truly great drives. He led from the start but a flat tyre on his Lotus meant he had to pit and he lost a whole lap to the leaders. When he came back out he drove out of his skin and made up an entire lap and amazingly took the lead again. Fuel pump problems on the last lap dropped him to third behind Surtees and Brabham but he had yet again proved his genius behind the wheel.

SEPTEMBER 11

The Gordon Murray designed McLaren-Honda car conquered almost all before it in the 1988 season, winning 15 out of 16 races that year in the hands of Ayrton Senna and Alain Prost. The only race it did not win was the Italian GP held on this day at Monza. Just weeks after Enzo Ferrari had passed away Gerhard Berger and Michele Alboreto took a Ferrari 1-2 at their home circuit to send the crowd wild.

Today in 1994 another famous team raced their last race. Johnny Herbert had the honour of being the last man to race a Lotus in F1. He qualified an amazing fourth on the grid for the Italian GP but in the race an accident and then engine failure put him out. The once dominant team went into receivership the next day.

SEPTEMBER 12

The Italian GP today in 1976 saw the sensational return to the cockpit of Niki Lauda just six weeks after the terrible accident at the Nurburgring which had so nearly claimed his life. Despite still being badly scarred and missing part of his ear the Austrian showed typical determination to get back behind the wheel of his Ferrari and try to claim the title that he was heading for before his crash. Even Ferrari were caught out by his decision and had to run an extra car for Carlos Reutemann who they had hired to drive in Lauda's stead. Lauda finished an incredible fourth, Reutemann ninth.

With Michael Schumacher out of the picture in 1999 thanks to his broken leg at Silverstone it looked like Mika Hakkinen might have a clear run to the World Championship. He arrived and took pole at Monza but in the race on this day he made an unforced error on lap 30 and crashed out. He was obviously distraught and was captured on camera sobbing in the trees at the side of the circuit.

SEPTEMBER 13

The 2007 F1 season was blighted by the so-called Stepney-gate scandal when disaffected Ferrari engineer Nigel Stepney was alleged to have passed information about the cars on to McLaren designer Mike Coughlan. On this day the World Motorsport Council announced McLaren were fined $100m and excluded them from the constructors' championship. McLaren drivers Lewis Hamilton and Fernando Alonso were not penalised.

Today in 2008 the drivers were hit by heavy rain in qualifying for the Italian GP at Monza and some coped better than others. The big surprise was Sebastian Vettel, the 21-year-old rookie in the Toro Rosso, who took pole position to become the youngest ever pole-sitter in F1. He said: 'Unbelievable. Incredible. I never dreamt of being on pole.'

SEPTEMBER 14

Double World Champion Mika Hakkinen announced today in 2001 that he would be taking a sabbatical year from Formula One, with fellow Finn Kimi Raikkonen set to replace him at McLaren. He said: 'Formula One has virtually been my whole life since I started karting in 1974. The intensity of my career has become increasingly difficult for those around me. I asked the team for a break which would be a good way to recharge my batteries and enjoy more time with my wife Erja and my son Hugo.' Mika never returned to the sport.

If Sebastian Vettel thought taking pole at Monza in 2008 was 'unbelievable', he went one better on this day when he took the victory in a rain-soaked race at the famous Italian track. Aided by the conditions but driving superbly, Vettel became the youngest ever F1 winner, stealing the crown from Fernando Alonso. It was also Toro Rosso's maiden win – a stunning achievement for what had been the perennial backmarker Minardi team for many years.

SEPTEMBER 15

The 1980s was a golden age for Formula One with many of the sport's top drivers all competing against each other. Ayrton Senna won the Belgian Grand Prix at Spa on this day in 1985 and he was followed home by Nigel Mansell, Alain Prost, Keke Rosberg and Nelson Piquet – all five were, or went on to become, World Champions.

Italian racing driver Alex Zanardi suffered a huge crash on this day in 2001 while racing in the Cart series in Germany. The former F1 driver who had stints with Jordan, Lotus and Williams, was very nearly killed and had to have both legs amputated. Not only did he survive but incredibly he was back racing again within two years.

SEPTEMBER 16

Graham Hill won the Italian Grand Prix on this day in 1962 in his BRM. It was his third victory of the season but was not quite enough to clinch him his first World Championship – he had to wait until the South African Grand Prix in December for that.

The events in America on September 11, 2001 touched everyone around the world and serious consideration was given to cancelling the Italian Grand Prix. In the end the race was held on this day, although it was understandably a sombre affair. Michael Schumacher seemed to be the most affected and even tried to organise a pact with the other drivers not to overtake at the first two corners but that was scuppered when Jacques Villeneuve refused. In the end Juan Pablo Montoya took his maiden F1 win while Schumi finished an uncharacteristic fourth. Ferrari boss Jean Todt said: 'For various reasons, his heart wasn't in it at this track,' while Schumi said simply, 'I'm glad this weekend is over.'

SEPTEMBER 17

When Damon Hill won the World Championship in 1996 he had effectively already been sacked by his Williams team and he ended up in an uncompetitive Arrows for the following season. Today in 1997 he announced he was leaving Arrows to sign for Jordan in a deal thought to be funded by the team's title sponsor Benson and Hedges. Damon said: 'My aim is to win races and challenge for the World Championship. Jordan has shown in 1997 that they can challenge for motorsport's greatest prize. This team is going to be a very strong force. The deal gives me the most competitive situation I could have.'

Honda is not the only carmaker to suddenly pull out of F1 in recent years and today in 2004 Ford announced it was pulling the plug on the Jaguar F1 team at the end of the season. The team was originally Stewart-Ford but Ford had taken control and re-branded it in 2000 amid much fanfare. Sadly the pomp was not backed up by results which were consistently miserable throughout the team's four-year existence.

SEPTEMBER 18

Olivier Panis announced his retirement from Formula One today in 2006, ending his 12-year spell in the sport. He made his debut with Ligier back in 1994, going on to take his first – and only – grand prix win in 1996 in Monaco for the French team. A shot at the 1997 title was ruined when he crashed and broke both legs at the Canadian GP but he returned to racing late in the season. After leaving Prost in 1999 he spent a year testing for McLaren before returning to a race seat, first with BAR and then Toyota.

At the end of the 2004 season Panis stopped racing for Toyota to become test driver for the team. It meant that 2005 was the first F1 season to feature no French drivers since 1966.

SEPTEMBER 19

Jackie Stewart won a rain-soaked Canadian Grand Prix today in 1971 at Mosport Park in his Tyrrell, on his way to his second World Championship. Ronnie Peterson was second for March but more impressive was American driver Mark Donohue who finished third in a McLaren on his Formula One debut.

Formula One has always had a difficult relationship with America. The USA has never really taken to it despite grands prix being held in numerous locations all over the country. In 2000 Indianapolis had a go, nearly ten years after the last GP was held in the States at Phoenix. To promote the race, on this day Eddie Irvine drove his Jaguar F1 car up Broadway in New York City in front of thousands of fans. Ever the bridesmaid, Johnny Herbert drove behind in a New York-style yellow taxi. Johnny said: 'The atmosphere was unbelievable. I knew we would create a fuss, but the turnout was overwhelming. It shows that the American public are really getting behind Formula One.'

SEPTEMBER 20

Jacky Ickx has won the Canadian Grand Prix twice on this day, both times leading home a 1-2 for his team. The first was in 1969 when, racing for Brabham, Ickx qualified in pole position and duelled with Jackie Stewart for the lead until they collided and Stewart was unable to get going again. Ickx won with Jack Brabham second. The leaders all lapped the hopeless local driver Al Pease at least four times before the marshals had had enough and black-flagged him. He remains the only driver in F1 history to be pulled put of a race for being too slow.

The following year Ickx won the race again, this time leading home Clay Regazzoni for a Ferrari 1-2. Al Pease did not take part.

SEPTEMBER 21

In the late 1940s the world was starting to try to return to normality after six years of war had ravaged most of Europe. Today in 1947 grand prix racing returned to France after a long interruption. Monaco-born Louis Chiron took victory at Lyons-Parilly in his Talbot-Lago car.

The Jenson Button contract saga rumbled on again today in 2005 when the British driver had to buy his way out of a contract he had signed to drive for Williams in 2006. After deciding he would rather stay with BAR Button was in something of a pickle and had to pay a fee to Frank Williams reported to be between £10m and £20m to get out of his deal. 'I regret the difficulties my decision has caused everyone involved,' said Button.

SEPTEMBER 22

The Williams team has twice won grands prix at Estoril in Portugal on this day, but in vastly different circumstances. In 1991 Nigel Mansell was fighting for the World Championship and after starting fourth had carved his way up to lead the race. On lap 29 he pitted for tyres and in just a few seconds his title hopes had evaporated. His right rear tyre was not on properly when he drove off and it detached from the car and rolled down the pitlane. Mansell stopped in the middle of the pitlane and was thumping the steering wheel in frustration as his mechanics came and stuck on a new wheel. Despite a storming drive back up to sixth, he was black-flagged for having his car worked on in the pitlane. His championship hopes were over for yet another year.

In 1996 the Williams car was the class of the field and Damon Hill and Jacques Villeneuve really only had each other to battle with. Villeneuve won to keep his faint championship hopes alive but Hill finished the job at the next race in Japan.

SEPTEMBER 23

American driver Peter Revson won two grands prix in his F1 career; the second was the Canadian race at Mosport Park on this day in 1973. It was a somewhat fortuitous victory as a mix up with the pace car (which was being used for the first time) on lap 33 allowed Revson to gain nearly a lap on much of the field. Nevertheless he won for McLaren but was killed the following year in testing for the South African Grand Prix.

Nigel Mansell triumphed in the Portuguese Grand Prix at Estoril on this day in 1990, finishing ahead of Ayrton Senna and Alain Prost on the podium. After the podium ceremony Nige made his way to the interview room standing up in an open top car, waving to the crowd when he hit his head on a steel beam. Murray Walker was waiting to interview him and in his haste to show the viewers the bump on Nigel's head Murray accidentally prodded it creating a clip that is wheeled out as one of the classic 'Murrayisms'.

SEPTEMBER 24

Mansell was also making waves in the 1989 Portuguese Grand Prix, held on this day. The Englishman missed his Ferrari pit box when he came in for a stop and, against the rules, reversed into it. He then ignored the inevitable black-flags and fought Senna for second place, before they collided and took each other out on lap 49. Gerhard Berger (Ferrari) won the race while Stefan Johansson came in third, scoring the only podium finish for the short-lived Onyx team. Pierluigi Martini led one lap of the GP – the only time a Minardi has ever led a race.

At the 1995 Portuguese GP David Coulthard beat his Williams-Renault colleague Damon Hill to pole position and then beat him and Michael Schumacher in the race. It was DC's first ever win in Formula One.

SEPTEMBER 25

Today in 2005 Fernando Alonso finished third in the Brazilian Grand Prix to claim the World Championship. At the time he became the youngest ever F1 World Champion although that record has now been taken by Lewis Hamilton. Alonso said after the race: 'I came from a country with no tradition in Formula One and I fought alone basically because I have not had any help from anybody all throughout my career. This is the maximum I can achieve in my life and career.'

The result meant the title had been wrestled away from Schumacher for the first time in five years. Although more race wins would follow for the Red Baron, he would never win the championship again.

SEPTEMBER 26

The European Grand Prix held at the Nurburgring on this day in 1999 was one of the most eventful and unpredictable in recent years as the wet/dry conditions caused havoc among the front-runners. Jordan driver Heinz-Harald Frentzen was putting together an unlikely title charge and had put his car on pole. In the race he was leading until an electronic gremlin ended his day and his title chances. After that the race was led by David Coulthard, Ralf Schumacher and Giancarlo Fisichella in succession but the rain or tyre problems put paid to their chances and Johnny Herbert, the unluckiest man in F1, had a dose of good luck for a change and drove calmly through the rain and the chaos to take a very popular and unexpected win. It was his third victory and the first for the Stewart team.

His teammate Rubens Barrichello joined him on the podium, finishing third. Eddie Irvine's race was ruined by a shockingly bad pitstop when his Ferrari crew could not find his fourth wheel. He was left sitting on the jack with only three wheels on his wagon for an age before they found it.

SEPTEMBER 27

Gilles Villeneuve was renowned for his never-say-die attitude to racing and he once again displayed that quality on this day in 1981 at his home grand prix at Montreal, Canada. In torrential rain, Gilles had severely damaged the front wing of his Ferrari. Rather than waste time by pitting to have it sorted out he drove on with the wing obscuring his view. Eventually it became detached and he drove to an impressive third place with the nose section of the car missing.

When Damon Hill was looking for a new team for the 1997 season he told the press he was talking to everyone except Minardi. In the end he joined the team second to Minardi in the list of all-time F1 losers. Today in 1996 the British driver surprised everyone when he announced he had signed for perennial backmarkers Arrows. Hill almost took a victory for the team at the Hungaroring but left after just one, winless season.

SEPTEMBER 28

History was made on this day in 2008 when Formula One held its first ever night race in Singapore. Bernie Ecclestone had always been keen on the idea as it meant viewers in Western Europe did not have to get up in the middle of the night to see the action. Thousands of high-powered lights lined the street circuit and the race saw an unexpected victory for Renault's Fernando Alonso, his first all season.

Ferrari scored another own goal during Felipe Massa's pitstop when they released him before the fuel rig had been detached. As he drove away he ripped the hose off the rig and drove down the pitlane dragging it along behind. He had to stop at the end of the pitlane as his mechanics raced the length of it, cheered on by their McLaren counterparts, to remove it.

SEPTEMBER 29

Two of the world's top drivers in two of the sport's best cars provided one of the most iconic and exciting scenes on a racetrack in living memory on this day in the Spanish Grand Prix of 1991 at Barcelona. Nigel Mansell in the Williams was charging through the field and was right behind Senna's McLaren going into the straight. Nigel made his move and the two great rivals were wheel-to-wheel, just millimetres apart at over 190 miles per hour. Neither driver wanted to yield but with sparks flying up from the underside of the cars, Mansell had the line into turn one and held the position before going on to win.

After the huge backlash against Ferrari team orders at the 2002 Austrian GP the subject was back with a vengeance today that same year at the US GP at Indianapolis. Utterly dominant, the Ferrari's were leading first and second but on the last corner Michael let Barrichello through into the lead. They crossed the line side by side, neither knowing who had won. Afterwards Schumi at first tried to claim he was trying to engineer a dead heat, but later changed his story saying it was payback for Austria. The gap between them was 0.011 seconds – the closest finish in F1 history.

SEPTEMBER 30

Everyone has their favourite 'Murrayism' from Murray Walker's countless gaffes over the years of his F1 commentary. Two of the best are surely: 'And we've had five races so far this year – Brazil, Argentina, Imola, Schumacher and Monaco,' and, 'It's Mansell! Mansell! Mansell! Nigel Mansell!' (It was Alain Prost).

Today in 2001, at the US Grand Prix, F1 fans heard Murray's familiar tones for the last time when he completed his last commentary on the sport for television, more than half a century after his did his first. As Murray once said: 'A sad ending, albeit a happy one.'

FORMULA ONE
On This Day

OCTOBER

OCTOBER 1

After a difficult 1990 season at Ferrari where he had been forced to play second fiddle to Alain Prost, Nigel Mansell announced he planned to retire from the sport. He was only persuaded to reverse this decision when Frank Williams offered him a drive for the following year. Mansell demanded number one status in the team and a host of other conditions, including a large retainer. Eventually a deal was struck and today in 1990 Nige signed the contract with the team that would make him World Champion in 1992.

Another Ferrari driver was winding his F1 career down on this day in 2006. Michael Schumacher, the German ace who had dominated Formula One for so long, took his final win today in the Chinese Grand Prix at Shanghai. It was his 91st victory – a record and an incredible 40 ahead of his nearest challenger, Alain Prost on 51.

OCTOBER 2

During the Second World War RAF Silverstone was a bomber base but it was discovered by racing enthusiasts soon afterwards and soon came to the attention of the Royal Automobile Club when they were looking for somewhere to host the British Grand Prix. With Donington Park and Brooklands out of action, Silverstone got the nod and on this day in 1948 the circuit hosted its first British GP. It was a great success with Luigi Villoresi winning from fellow Italian Alberto Ascari, both in Maseratis.

In 1977 Niki Lauda won a very popular second World Championship, having battled back to form and fitness after he was very nearly killed in the German GP in 1976. Today in 1977 Lauda drove his final race for Ferrari in the United States Grand Prix at Watkins Glen. Having wrapped up the title the previous race he came home in fourth place but would never drive for the Prancing Horse again, who replaced him with unknown Gilles Villeneuve.

OCTOBER 3

Before he calmed down in Formula One, James Hunt was known as 'Hunt the Shunt' for his tendency to crash. Today in 1970 he took part in the Formula Three Daily Express Trophy race at Crystal Palace. During the race he battled hard against Dave Morgan and eventually the pair tangled and both crashed out. Hunt earned himself a ticking off from the organisers by jumping out of his car, running over to Morgan and pushing him over in a fury.

Seven years to the day later and Hunt was in the big time and contesting the World Championship with McLaren. Today in 1976 he won the Canadian Grand Prix at Mosport Park after taking pole the day before. His win meant he closed the gap to Niki Lauda in the World Championship to just eight points. He went on to win the title at the final round in Japan.

OCTOBER 4

A month after championship leader Jochen Rindt had been killed at Monza the F1 circus arrived at Watkins Glen for the US Grand Prix on this day in 1970. Only Jacky Ickx could take the title from Rindt but he needed to win both the US and the Mexican GPs to do it. He took pole but a mechanical problem ended his race and his title hopes. Brazilian Emerson Fittipaldi, promoted to team leader at Lotus after Rindt's death, took his first victory to ensure Rindt won the title – the only posthumous World Champion in the history of the sport.

The blood-red Ferrari cars are the most instantly recognisable on the F1 grid but today in 1964 the cars ran in the United States GP in an unfamiliar blue and white colour scheme. Enzo Ferrari was in dispute with the Italian national automobile club and so entered his cars in United States colours rather than Italian red. His lead driver John Surtees finished second behind Graham Hill.

OCTOBER 5

Most Formula One team owners are really frustrated drivers themselves and today in 1919 Enzo Ferrari himself entered his very first motor race. Aged just 21, Enzo finished 11th in the Parmo-Poggia di Berceto hill climb in a Costruzioni Meccaniche Nazionali (CMN) car. Two years later he joined Alfa Romeo and soon found he was better employed running the racing team than driving. After World War Two he decided to found his own company and Scuderia Ferrari was born.

Today in 1969 Austrian driver Jochen Rindt took his first Formula One victory in the United States Grand Prix at Watkins Glen. The win had been coming all season as Rindt in the Lotus had already started on pole four times, led in five races and had back-to-back podiums in the previous two races. He took pole again and battled with Jackie Stewart until the Scot retired with engine failure.

OCTOBER 6

The 1973 United States GP at Watkins Glen was to be triple World Champion Jackie Stewart's last race. The plan was for Stewart's understudy Francois Cevert to become team leader at Tyrrell after JYS stood down. Tragically that would never happen because on this day, in the practice session, Cevert crashed heavily into the barriers at The Esses and was killed instantly. After all Stewart's safety campaigning it was ironic that it was his own teammate and apprentice who had paid the price.

Peter Warr, team manager at Lotus once said of Nigel Mansell: 'He'll never win a grand prix as long as I have hole in my arse.' Today in 1985 Warr had to eat those rather disgusting words when Nige took his first F1 victory at the 72nd attempt. The mustachioed master took his win on British soil, at Brands Hatch in the European Grand Prix. Alain Prost finished fourth in the race to win his first World Championship.

OCTOBER 7

Today in 1979 Gilles Villeneuve showed off his legendary skills by outclassing the whole field in the wet at Watkins Glen. In a rain sodden Friday practice Villeneuve stunned the whole paddock with his lap times – reported to be between nine and 11 seconds faster than anyone else. Jody Scheckter recalled: 'I scared myself rigid that day. I thought I had to be quickest. Then I saw Gilles' time and — I still don't really understand how it was possible.'

Lewis Hamilton has proved he too has what it takes to drive in the wet when others can find no grip and today in 2007 the young charger looked like he had the Chinese GP and the World Championship in the bag when, on his way into the pits he slid off the track and beached his McLaren in the gravel. He was out and at the next race he lost the championship by just one point to Kimi Raikkonen.

OCTOBER 8

Gilles Villeneuve once said: 'If someone said to me that you can have three wishes, my first would have been to get into racing, my second to be in Formula 1, my third to drive for Ferrari.' Perhaps his fourth wish would have been to win his home race, and that's what he did today in 1978 when he triumphed in the Canadian GP at Montreal for Ferrari – his first ever F1 win.

When Jody Scheckter won the World Championship in 1979 no one imagined it would be more than two decades before a Ferrari driver repeated the feat. Michael Schumacher finally did it on this day in 2000 when he beat title rival Mika Hakkinen to win the final race of the season at Suzuka. Schumi said: 'I never thought I was never going to win another championship, but every year it doesn't happen, it gets longer and longer and you get more and more upset. To finally do it is simply great.'

OCTOBER 9

In 1976 James Hunt took time out of his title-winning season to enter a Formula Atlantic race in Canada at Trois-Rivières. He was soundly beaten by a young local driver named Gilles Villeneuve. Hunt returned to Europe and immediately recommended Villeneuve to his McLaren team who signed him up for a couple of races in 1977. Soon Enzo Ferrari decided he wanted Villeneuve and today in 1977 he made his debut for the team that he would stay with for the rest of his career – fittingly at his home race, the Canadian GP at Mosport Park.

The Japanese GP at Suzuka today in 2005 was a belter of a race remembered for two ballsy overtaking manoeuvres. The first saw the new World Champion Fernando Alonso show he wasn't afraid of anyone or any corner when he took Michael Schumacher on the outside around the famous 130R corner. Brave stuff. Not to be outdone, McLaren's Kimi Raikkonen battled to an impressive victory after starting 17th. He took the lead on the last lap at turn one when he too went around the outside, this time of Giancarlo Fisichella in the Renault.

OCTOBER 10

In 2001 Honda decided to supply works engines to both Jordan and BAR to try to ensure success with at least one team. It was rumoured that the more successful team would win Honda engines for the long term. Never one to miss a trick, Eddie Jordan decided to sign up Japanese driver and Honda favourite Takuma Sato to drive for his team. Sato signed on this day in 2001.

Sato has still not managed to win a grand prix but today in 2004 he had a decent showing in his home event, the Japanese GP at Suzuka. By now with BAR-Honda the local man finished fourth to send the crowd home reasonably happy.

OCTOBER 11

After winning his third and last title with McLaren in 1991, Ayrton Senna was hungry for more success but a downturn in the fortunes of the team held him back. In 1992 he was completely outclassed by Nigel Mansell and Williams who had got the upper hand on McLaren. This continued with Prost in 1993 and Senna was desperate to get into the Williams car for 1994. Eventually he got his wish, and pushed Prost into retirement in the process. Williams announced that they had signed Senna on this day in 1993. Senna said: 'It is like a dream come true.' It was to turn from dream to nightmare for Senna who was killed at Imola in only his third race with the team.

The A1GP series, known as the world cup of motorsport because each team represents their nation, became an all-Italian affair in one respect today in 2007 when it was announced that Ferrari would be supplying all the engines for the cars from 2008.

OCTOBER 12

All the attention was on Nigel Mansell at the Mexican GP on this day in 1986 where a good result could win him the championship with a race to spare. Mansell made a bad start and could only manage fifth but the headlines were stolen by Austrian driver Gerhard Berger who took his, and the Benetton team's, first win after a clever tyre strategy on his Pirelli rubber outfoxed his Goodyear-shod rivals. After stints with Ferrari and McLaren, Berger returned to Benetton in 1996 and he book-ended the team's existence neatly by taking their last ever win at the Hockenheimring in 1997.

Yet another F1 record tumbled today in 2003 at the Japanese GP when Michael Schumacher won his sixth World Championship, eclipsing the previous record of five set by Juan Manuel Fangio nearly half a century earlier.

OCTOBER 13

After coming so close to the title in 1994, Damon Hill looked to be cruising to the championship in 1996 until his rookie teammate Jacques Villeneuve started a late surge which threatened Hill's dreams. It was on this day, at the Japanese GP at Suzuka that Hill held his nerve to win the race and the title. The British fans who had got up early to watch the race were not disappointed and as he crossed the finish line an emotional Murray Walker said: 'And I've got to stop because I've got a lump in my throat.' Damon, son of Graham Hill, became the first and so far only son of a World Champion to win the title himself.

The race in Japan was also the racing swansong of Martin Brundle. Today in 2001 ITV announced that Brundle was to be joined in the commentary box the following season by pitlane reporter James Allen who was chosen to replace the retiring Murray Walker.

OCTOBER 14

Jean Alesi, the French-Sicilian driver who was immensely talented but often seemed to find himself in the wrong car, brought his Formula One career to a close at the Japanese Grand Prix on this day in 2001. Jean pulled out of a move to Williams in 1990 to instead sign for Ferrari. It was a classic case of his heart ruling his head: the Williams drive could have made him World Champion, while the Ferrari was never really competitive in his time there and he only ever won one grand prix. Sadly Jean was not even able to complete his last GP after his Jordan was hit by Kimi Raikkonen's Sauber and he had to retire on lap five.

Unbeknown to anyone at the time, the Japanese GP in 2001 was also the last race the Prost team competed in. The team, run by Alesi's old Ferrari teammate Alain Prost, was unable to raise the necessary sponsorship for the 2002 season and folded in the close season.

OCTOBER 15

The 1983 Formula One season had an exciting finale on this day when the teams and drivers gathered at Kyalami for the South African Grand Prix – the final round of the championship. All was still to play for as Alain Prost (Renault), Nelson Piquet (Brabham) and Rene Arnoux (Ferrari) were all still in contention for the title – the first three-way battle since 1974. Arnoux was the first to blink when his Ferrari engine blew on lap nine; and Prost was out on lap 35 also with engine trouble. Piquet finished third and so won his second drivers' title by two points over Prost.

Arnoux was not helped in his efforts by some over-eager marshals who had come to his aid when his car broke down on the track in practice. In pushing the car off the track they succeeded in pushing one of the wheels over Arnoux's foot leaving him hobbling around for the rest of the weekend.

OCTOBER 16

The European Grand Prix at Jerez on this day in 1994 saw the final F1 appearance of Andrea de Cesaris. Nicknamed 'Andrea de Crasheris' for his frequent misadventures, the Italian driver holds some of the most unwanted records in the sport. With 208 grands prix under his belt he has the most race starts without a win, and the record for the most successive non-finishes with 18 across 1985 and 1986. In the 1987 season he only managed to finish two out of 16 races – also a record. Indeed, he also holds the record for DNFs, 135 in his career meaning he only ever finished 73 of his 208 races.

Fernando Alonso has an altogether better F1 record and it got even better at the Chinese Grand Prix today in 2005 when he led home Giancarlo Fisichella in a Renault 1-2 to win the first ever constructors' championship for the French marque.

OCTOBER 17

As the 1999 season drew to its climax Michael Schumacher returned from his broken leg for the Malaysian GP on this day to help Eddie Irvine's title bid. His enforced lay-off had dulled none of his talent and Schumi was instantly quick. For once, as Murray Walker would say, the boot was on the other Schumacher and Michael was on the other side of team orders for the first time. He waved Irvine through in the final laps so the Ulsterman could win, with his rival Mika Hakkinen in third.

It set up a thrilling title decider for the final race of the season in Japan; or so it seemed. Just hours after the race had finished the FIA announced Irvine and Schumacher had been disqualified because of a minor rule infringement of part of the car's bodywork. The result was that Hakkinen inherited the win and was named provisional World Champion. At appeal a week later the decision was overturned and both Ferraris were reinstated in the results. Hakkinen then had to race to win his second title.

OCTOBER 18

Nigel Mansell won the Mexican Grand Prix today in 1987, but he was not the first man to cross the finish line. He actually came home behind his Williams teammate Nelson Piquet but was still declared the winner. Confused? Mansell had been leading until Derek Warwick had a big accident and the race was stopped on 30 laps. The restarted race was decided on aggregate times. Piquet took the lead at the restart but Mansell simply kept up close behind him so there was no way the Brazilian could win.

Today in 2008 the battle for the World Championship was hotting up but Lewis Hamilton kept his cool to take pole position for the Chinese GP at Shanghai. He took victory the following day with rival Felipe Massa taking second to set up a tense championship decider in the last race in Brazil.

OCTOBER 19

Stirling Moss and Mike Hawthorn were locked in an intense title battle in 1958 that was set to be decided at the last race, the Moroccan GP on this day. Moss needed to set the fastest lap and win the race to stand any chance of World Championship glory and he kept his side of the bargain by storming to victory. But it was not enough as Hawthorn took second place and with it the title. He became Britain's first ever World Champion and within a few days he had announced his retirement aged just 29.

It was not such a happy day for another British driver, Stuart Lewis-Evans. One of Moss's teammates in the Vanwall team, his engine blew up on lap 42 and after oil was sprayed everywhere he caught fire. He jumped out but he had suffered very serious burns and despite being flown back to a specialist burns unit in the UK he died in hospital six days later.

OCTOBER 20

Formula One lost yet another star today in 1978, but Swiss driver Gunnar Nilsson, winner of the 1977 Belgian Grand Prix, was not killed in a crash, but died of cancer aged just 29.

The Suzuka circuit in Japan hosted the championship decider in 1991 with Ayrton Senna and Nigel Mansell both in contention. Mansell needed to win to take the title but he could only take second on the grid behind Senna. Senna's McLaren teammate Gerhard Berger beat them both into the first corner and raced off. Mansell was stuck and desperate to get past Senna but on lap ten he went off and was out. Senna had won his third and final World Championship. He set off after Berger and easily overtook him with the Austrian suffering tyre problems. There was still time for a final gesture when Senna let Berger through to win at the final corner as a thank you for his friend's help.

OCTOBER 21

Today in 1990 Senna was having one of his epic title battles with Prost at Suzuka and the Brazilian had taken pole. He wanted the pole position on the grid changed to the clean side of the track but when his request was refused he was furious and thought the officials were favouring his rival. He decided he would not lift off at the first corner come what may. In the race Prost did indeed get a better start on the clean side of the track but, as he had promised, Senna did not give an inch going into the first corner and they were both off and out of the race. Senna was champion; Prost was livid.

The 2007 season was memorable not only for Lewis Hamilton's stunning debut but also the three-way title battle that was only decided at the final round in Brazil on this day. Outsider Kimi Raikkonen won in his Ferrari to beat Hamilton and Alonso to the crown.

OCTOBER 22

Suzuka was the setting for another controversial Senna/Prost battle on this day in 1989. Senna needed to win to keep his title hopes alive and he duly took pole, but Prost took the lead at the start. On lap 46 Senna made his move on Prost at the chicane. The two hit each other and slid off. Prost got out of the car thinking the title was his but Senna got a push from the marshals and rejoined the race. He drove superbly to catch and pass Alessandro Nannini (Benetton) for the lead and took the chequered flag. But he never made it to the podium as the stewards disqualified him for missing the chicane. Nannini was given the victory and Prost was champion.

Senna took his last victory at his home race at Interlagos in 1993. The fanatical Brazilian crowd had to wait until this day in 2006 for the next Brazilian winner when Felipe Massa triumphed for Ferrari.

OCTOBER 23

For the final round of the 1977 season the Japanese GP was held at Fuji on this day. James Hunt took his tenth and final victory in the McLaren although his title rival from the previous season Niki Lauda had already wrapped up the World Championship. The race was marred by another tragic accident when Gilles Villeneuve's Ferrari hit Ronnie Peterson's Tyrrell and cartwheeled off the track. Although Villeneuve was unhurt a marshal and a photographer were killed.

As well as being Hunt's last F1 win it was also the last for the McLaren team for four long years. The team would not reach the top step of the podium until Ron Dennis took control and John Watson won the British GP in July 1981.

OCTOBER 24

Despite missing part of the 1976 season after the terrible crash at the Nurburgring that nearly killed him, Niki Lauda was still in the championship hunt going into the final round at Mount Fuji in Japan. The rain was so heavy there were calls to cancel the race but it went ahead, although Lauda pulled out after just one lap claiming it was too dangerous. Englishman James Hunt finished third to win the title.

Eddie Irvine announced himself to Formula One today in 1993 at the Japanese GP at Suzuka. Driving a Jordan in his first ever F1 race the Ulsterman was trying to score points and unlapped himself by overtaking an incredulous Ayrton Senna. After the race Senna was livid and hunted Irvine down in the Jordan motorhome. The two had a heated exchange before Senna decided actions speak louder than words and punched the young driver in the face, giving Irv the Swerve a good story to tell at the pub that night.

OCTOBER 25

Graham Hill, Jim Clark and John Surtees were in with a shout of the title going into the season-deciding Mexican GP on this day in 1964. Even in the closing stages of the race Clark looked likely to win his second title until his Lotus engine seized up with just one lap remaining. Surtees finished second and took the World Championship. He became the first and so far only motorcycling World Champion to win the title on four wheels as well.

The whole F1 paddock was astonished today in 1997 when the qualifying session for the showdown title decider at Jerez produced a bizarre result. Title protagonists Jacques Villeneuve and Michael Schumacher plus Heinz-Harald Frentzen set identical fastest lap times to a margin of one thousandth of a second. It has never happened before or since.

OCTOBER 26

One of the most exciting races of the eighties was held at Adelaide on this day in 1986. The Australian GP would decide whether Nigel Mansell, Nelson Piquet or Alain Prost won the title. Prost's chances looked to be gone when a puncture forced him to pit to have his wheel changed but then fate intervened. As Mansell was battling with Piquet, wheel to wheel at 200 miles per hour down the main straight, Mansell's left rear tyre exploded spectacularly, along with his title hopes. Piquet had to pit to check for debris and Prost won the title.

The 1997 title was also decided on this day, this time at Jerez in Spain. When Jacques Villeneuve made his overtaking move on Michael Schumacher the German driver turned in on the Williams in an attempted repeat of his move on Damon Hill back in 1994. This time Schumi got it wrong and ended up beaching his Ferrari in the gravel trap while Villeneuve was able to continue and take the World Championship. Schumacher was later stripped of all his points for the season for his infamous manoeuvre.

OCTOBER 27

Jim Clark wrapped up another flag-to-flag victory today in 1963 when he stuck his Lotus on pole for the Mexican Grand Prix in Mexico City and then dominated the race to win by a minute and a half. It was his sixth win of the season which meant he equalled Fangio's record for championship wins in a single season with a race to spare. In December he won the South African Grand Prix at East London to take the record.

While Clark was out at the front on his own in the Mexican GP his rival Jack Brabham had a far more interesting race. He had started 10th on the grid but produced a great drive to work his way up to second before the chequered flag fell.

OCTOBER 28

Juan Manuel Fangio won his first World Championship on this day in 1951 when he took victory in his Alfa Romeo in the Spanish Grand Prix at the Padralbes circuit in Barcelona. He went into the race, the final round of the season, two points ahead of his Ferrari rival Alberto Ascari in the standings. A bad choice of tyres by the Ferrari team meant Ascari could only finish fourth and the title was Fangio's.

After the race it was announced that Alfa Romeo was withdrawing from the sport with immediate effect. The car and much of the technology the team used was getting extremely dated and when the Italian government refused the additional funding the team needed to keep pace with the emerging Ferrari team, they decided to withdraw on a high. The Alfa Romeo name was not seen again in Formula One until the 1970s. New World Champion Fangio was left without a drive for the 1952 season and suffered a broken neck in a crash during a one-off race with Maserati at Monza. He returned to F1 full-time in 1953 with Maserati.

OCTOBER 29

Having won his second World Championship with Benetton at the Pacific Grand Prix held at Aida, Japan, Michael Schumacher showed he was not on cruise control in the next race held on this day in 1995, the Japanese Grand Prix at the Suzuka circuit. He dominated the weekend taking pole and the win which, with teammate Johnny Herbert taking third, meant Benetton won the constructors' title as well.

Suzuka has always been one of Mika Hakkinen's favourite tracks but his second place in the race that day was a remarkable achievement for the Finn who was still recovering from an appendicitis operation which had kept him out of the previous round.

OCTOBER 30

The 1988 season was one of the great year-long battles between two of the greatest rivals the sport has ever seen. Alain Prost and Ayrton Senna, both driving the dominant McLaren-Honda, were in great form but Senna was determined to win his first title at the Japanese GP on this day. Senna had pole but unbelievably stalled at the start and watched as 13 cars shot past him. He managed to bump start his car and set off in pursuit of Prost. The Brazilian needed to win to take the title and after fighting his way through the field he took the lead on lap 28, never to surrender it. Formula One had a new World Champion.

Jos 'the Boss' Verstappen was certainly not feeling very bossy today in 2000 when he was found guilty of assault by a Belgian court. The charge related to an incident in 1998 when a man ended up with a fractured skull after a fight. The Dutch driver was spared jail and given a suspended sentence.

OCTOBER 31

When Michael Schumacher broke his leg in 1999 Eddie Irvine stepped up to the mantle for Ferrari to try to win the World Championship. Suddenly he went from understudy to leading role and he did better than many expected and was still in contention for the title going into the last race of the season at Suzuka, Japan on this day. It proved a bridge too far on one of title rival Mika Hakkinen's favourite tracks. Eddie could only qualify fifth while Mika started second on the grid. The Finn drove a perfect race to take the victory and win his second World Championship in as many years. Irv the Swerve was third in his last race for Ferrari.

It was also the last grand prix for 1996 World Champion Damon Hill. The Englishman had been struggling for much of the season and speculation had been rife that he would not see it out. He did so but his heart was clearly not in it anymore. He retired from the race and the sport on lap 21 citing handling problems with his Jordan.

FORMULA ONE
On This Day

NOVEMBER

NOVEMBER 1

After losing out on the title after a puncture put him out of the race in Australia in 1986, Nigel Mansell was once again in contention for the championship in 1987. His Williams teammate and title rival Nelson Piquet was 12 points ahead of Mansell going into the penultimate round at Suzuka on this day. Sadly for Nigel a big crash on this day in practice ruled him out of the race, handing the title to Piquet.

For all his talent Michael Schumacher was not above the occasional lapse in concentration. Today in 1998 Schumi stalled his Ferrari while on pole for the championship showdown with Mika Hakkinen at the final round at Suzuka. He had to start from the back of the grid and Hakkinen drove off to win the race and his first drivers' title.

NOVEMBER 2

When Fernando Alonso signed for McLaren he was already a double World Champion and was expecting the whole team to be behind his 2007 championship charge. When Lewis Hamilton started giving him a run for his money Fernando was not happy with the team's equal-status policy and the relationship between him and the team quickly soured. It was no surprise when his departure from the team was announced on this day in 2007. He said: 'Since I was a boy I had always wanted to drive for McLaren, but sometimes in life things do not work out.'

There has surely never been a more exciting climax to an F1 season than today in 2008 when Lewis Hamilton clinched the title on the last corner of the last lap of the last grand prix of the season. His rival Felipe Massa had done all he could by winning his home race and Lewis was only sixth going into the last few corners when he needed fifth to take the title. He took the place just yards before the finish line when he overtook Timo Glock.

NOVEMBER 3

The shortest and surely the most dangerous grand prix ever was held on this day in 1991 at Adelaide, Australia. The rain was lashing down but organisers decided the race would go ahead. As Senna, who had already won the championship, led the pack away at the start it was clear just how wet it was as the cameras struggled to even see the cars through the spray. Cars were spinning all over the track including those of Nicola Larini, Thierry Boutsen and Jean Alesi which were strewn across the start/finish straight. At one terrifying moment Nigel Mansell was shaping up to overtake Senna on the straight unable to see the stranded cars because of the spray. At the last moment he saw them and backed off but the conditions continued to worsen and soon Senna was waving his arms furiously at the officials signalling that the race should be stopped. Eventually they agreed and it was red-flagged after just 14 laps. The weather got no better so it was not restarted.

Three-time World Champion Nelson Piquet was particularly upset by the event's cancellation as it was his last race in the sport.

NOVEMBER 4

The 1990 Australian Grand Prix was run on this day at Adelaide. It was the 500th race of the Formula One World Championship since the series began at Silverstone back in 1950. Nelson Piquet won the milestone race for the Benetton team.

Flavio Briatore and Bernie Ecclestone's takeover of Queens Park Rangers FC was not the first time F1 bosses had been linked with the beautiful game. Today in 2001 the Williams team issued a statement denying Sir Frank Williams was about to launch a £23m takeover of Newcastle United. Sir Frank was born in Newcastle and already owned a small stake in the club, and had been spotted meeting with then Newcastle chairman Freddy Shepherd. The Williams team said the meeting was purely a personal visit.

NOVEMBER 5

The 1989 World Championship was settled at Suzuka when Prost and Senna collided and Prost won his third title. The last race of that season, the Australian Grand Prix, was held today at Adelaide. The conditions were so wet as to be treacherous and cancelling it was a distinct possibility. In the end it went ahead but Prost refused to race. The rest of the field did race and Senna had a healthy lead when he crashed into the back of Martin Brundle's Brabham because of the poor visibility. Eventually Thierry Boutsen won the rain-soaked race for Williams.

It was the last appearance in Formula One for veteran driver Rene Arnoux. The Frenchman had racked up seven wins in 149 starts in the sport.

NOVEMBER 6

The 1994 season was coming towards its conclusion today at Suzuka in the Japanese GP, the penultimate round of the championship. Damon Hill needed to win to keep his title hopes alive but Michael Schumacher took pole ahead of the Englishman. The race started in the wet but the rain got worse and worse until drivers were spinning off the track. Martin Brundle went off in his McLaren and hit some marshals who were attending to another car. One of them suffered a broken leg and the race was red flagged. After some discussion among the drivers the race restarted behind the safety car and Damon Hill drove a great race to win ahead of Schumacher.

The result meant the championship would go down to the wire as Schumacher took a one point lead to the final race of the season, the Australian Grand Prix at Adelaide – a race that would go down in infamy when Schumi drove into Hill to take him out of the race.

NOVEMBER 7

After six years with McLaren Ayrton Senna had signed to race for Williams in 1994. The Australian Grand Prix at Adelaide today in 1993 was his last race for McLaren and he wanted to go out on a high. He did so by taking pole position – the first time Williams had not got pole all season – and then drove a masterful race to win. Not only was it his last win for McLaren, but it would turn out to be his last ever Formula One victory when he was killed the following year.

World Champion Alain Prost came second in his Williams in his last ever grand prix. On the podium Senna shook his old rival's hand and pulled him up to the top step in an emotional scene. It was the last time either man would stand on the rostrum; their intense rivalry was finally at an end.

NOVEMBER 8

After watching his rivals at Williams dominate Formula One throughout the nineties Ron Dennis had had enough and decided to try to lure away Williams' chief designer and renowned aerodynamics whiz Adrian Newey, by reportedly offering him a big salary and shares in McLaren – something not on offer at Williams. Today in 1996 Newey decided not to turn up for work at Williams and eventually he negotiated his way out of his contract with the Grove-based team and joined McLaren where he designed the cars that returned them back to the front of the grid.

Nine years to the day later in 2005 Red Bull Racing announced that Newey would be joining the team in 2006 as Chief Technical Officer. It was something of a coup for the midfield team to lure away one of the sport's top designers after eight years at McLaren which saw Newey-designed cars twice win the World Championship with Mika Hakkinen.

NOVEMBER 9

After the McLaren 'Spygate' scandal that rocked F1 in 2007 the last thing the sport needed was another controversy but today in 2007 the Renault ream were forced to deny they too had been using data from another team, namely McLaren. At an FIA hearing the following month Renault were found guilty of breaching the same sporting regulations as McLaren had, but unlike McLaren, the team was not penalised.

Lewis Hamilton claimed there was no personal problem between him and Fernando Alonso despite the acrimony between the Spaniard and the McLaren team. At a Mercedes-Benz promotional event today in 2008 Lewis said: 'I don't think there was a particular dispute between us. We've greeted each other when we've met each other at the track – we've always respected each other.'

NOVEMBER 10

David Coulthard often spoke of the closeness between his team boss Ron Dennis and his McLaren driver Mika Hakkinen. That bond was in part due to events that occurred on this day in 1995. In Friday practice for the Australian GP at Adelaide Mika suffered a tyre failure that catapulted him into a wall at tremendous speed. Unconscious and seriously injured, the medical crew saved his life by giving him an emergency tracheotomy at the side of the track. He was rushed to hospital with the rest of the paddock fearing the worst, but happily he survived. Over the winter he recovered and began testing the car again. His two World Championships in 1998 and 1999 were the culmination of a remarkable recovery for the Flying Finn.

Today in 2008 Ferrari president Luca di Montezemolo revealed that he was so angry when Felipe Massa lost the World Championship to Lewis Hamilton in the final moments of the Brazilian GP that he smashed his television set. 'I broke the television,' he said. 'When a television breaks it makes a terrible bang. My daughter in the other room was given an awful fright.'

NOVEMBER 11

Today in 1997 was judgement day for Michael Schumacher as the FIA World Motorsport Council (WMSC) sat to discuss what punishment to mete out to the German for his attempt to drive championship rival Jacques Villeneuve off the track at the final race of the season. He could have been banned for a season or fined but instead the FIA merely excluded him from the 1997 championship standings and made him participate in a road safety campaign. The press were outraged at the weak penalty. Even German tabloid *Das Bild* described it as 'crazy'.

The WMSC also passed judgement on another matter from the same race. Williams and McLaren were accused by *The Times* newspaper of colluding to engineer the result but the WMSC threw the case out. 'It is quite clear that the result of the race was not fixed,' said Max Mosley, FIA President. 'There was no arrangement between McLaren and Williams that Mika Hakkinen was going to win.'

NOVEMBER 12

Damon Hill took his 14th grand prix win in Adelaide on this day in 1995. It was too late to have any effect on the championship which Michael Schumacher had already wrapped up but it was significant for the margin of Damon's victory. He was a full two laps clear of the second-placed man Olivier Panis in the Ligier – only the second time in the history of the World Championship this has happened. The first was May 4, 1969 at the Spanish GP when Jackie Stewart beat Bruce McLaren by the same huge margin. Hill was aided by some collisions behind him as his Williams teammate David Coulthard hit the pitwall, while Schumacher and Jean Alesi ran into each other with both forced to retire.

This was also the last Australian GP to be held at Adelaide, which had hosted the event for 11 years. The race moved to Melbourne the following season.

NOVEMBER 13

Michael Schumacher was supremely talented but also had a dark side which F1 fans saw for the first time today in 1994 at the title showdown at Adelaide. Unseen by his rival Damon Hill, Schumi made an error and damaged his own car. Hill rounded the corner and went to overtake the German who turned in on the Williams driver. Schumacher was out and got out of his car and waited anxiously to see if Hill was able to continue running. Hill's car was too badly damaged and he had to retire, handing Schumacher his first World Championship by just one point. Schumacher was pilloried by the British press and forever cast as the pantomime villain in the minds of Damon Hill's fans.

With Hill and Schumacher both out Nigel Mansell picked up the win in the second Williams. It was the old charger's last F1 victory.

NOVEMBER 14

The first ever London to Brighton car run was staged on this day in 1896. Dubbed the Emancipation Run, it was organised by Henry Lawson to celebrate the passing of the *Locomotives on the Highway Act* which raised the speed limit for cars from 4mph to 14mph and abolished the need for a man to walk in front of vehicles. The requirement to have a man waving a red flag in front of a car was actually abolished in 1878 but the *Locomotive Act* was still widely known as the Red Flag Act and a red flag was symbolically burned at the start of the run. More than 30 motorists set out from London that day but only 14 of the starters made it to Brighton and there remains some suspicion that one of those was actually taken by train and then covered with mud before crossing the finish line.

The run was staged again in 1927 and has run every year since, save for the war years, and is the longest-running motoring event in the world.

NOVEMBER 15

With Nelson Piquet having already won the World Championship at the previous round thanks to Nigel Mansell's accident, the Australian GP at Adelaide on this day in 1987 was an end of term affair. Ferrari's Gerhard Berger was brimming with confidence following his win in the last race and he took pole position ahead of Alain Prost's McLaren. Berger got away well and led from start to finish to pick up his second consecutive win, while behind him Piquet, Prost, Senna and Michele Alboreto battled for second place. Alboreto eventually won the duel to secure Ferrari's first 1-2 for more than two years.

The race was the final outing in a Williams for Brazilian World Champion Nelson Piquet. He moved to Lotus for the 1988 season but never won another title.

NOVEMBER 16

Today in 1991 Fiat chairman Gianni Agnelli made Luca di Montezemolo president of Ferrari, which had been in the doldrums for some years. He immediately set about reviving the Prancing Horse and set a target of winning the World Championship. It took the team nearly ten years to do it but in 2000 the goal was achieved. He is now also chairman of Fiat.

The Ligier name disappeared from motor racing when Alain Prost bought the team in 1997 and changed its name to Prost Grand Prix. Today in 2004 Ligier was back when the company launched its first racing car for eight years. The new car, the Automobiles Ligier JS47 was designed to run in Formula Three. Guy Ligier said: 'We've been working on this project for around 10 months. We have been focusing carefully on designing efficient aerodynamics, transmission and suspension. I wanted to build a fast, reliable racing car. It's always great to be involved in the birth of a new car. Taking the car from concept to creation is always special as is hearing that on track it behaves like our simulations predicted.'

NOVEMBER 17

A political row was brewing in 1997 after Tony Blair's new government exempted Formula One from a ban on tobacco sponsorship. It then emerged that Bernie Ecclestone had donated £1m to the Labour Party before the election, and that Blair had met with Ecclestone and Max Mosley at Downing Street in October. Today in 1997 Mr Blair was forced to apologise over his handling of the incident and promised to return Ecclestone's money, but denied any wrongdoing. He said: 'I had absolutely no intention of changing the policy for Bernie Ecclestone.'

On this day in 2004 it was announced that Juan Pablo Montoya would leave Williams and race for McLaren in 2005. 'The team is consistently a strong World Championship contender and has a fantastic heritage,' he said. 'It's a great opportunity for me and I'm really looking forward to the first time I will be able to drive one of their cars. To join them is an amazing challenge and experience which I plan to fully enjoy.'

NOVEMBER 18

On this day in 2008 Bernie Ecclestone horrified many F1 fans when he was quoted by *The Times* newspaper suggesting that a new medals-type system of scoring was to be introduced to the sport. 'Everybody understands gold medals and silver and bronze,' he said. 'Nearly all sports are done that way. The whole point will be, when they get to Melbourne for the first race, the guys will want to leave there with a gold medal. They don't want to leave with ten, eight or six points. I'm absolutely 100 percent sure it's the right way to go, it'll get them (the drivers) overtaking.'

Former team boss Eddie Jordan called the scheme 'nonsense' and said: 'He thinks people are only interested in winning the races. I'm sorry, but there's just not enough thought put into this. For Bernie Ecclestone to say it's coming with the full approval of all the teams, I simply don't believe it.'

JUAN PABLO MONTOYA BID FAREWELL TO WILLIAMS IN NOVEMBER 2004

NOVEMBER 19

One of the best ways for any aspiring F1 drivers to get noticed is to win the Macau Grand Prix – the most important race on the Formula 3 calendar held in the former Portuguese territory in China. Many F1 stars have won the race over the years including Ayrton Senna, Michael Schumacher and David Coulthard. Today in 1995 Ralf Schumacher took victory in the showpiece event. He was in F1 with Jordan within two years.

The BAR team were celebrating today in 2004 when Honda bought around 45 per cent of the company from owners BAT. It signalled Honda's serious intentions for their F1 programme but did lead to the departure of team boss Dave Richards who had been brought in to run things by BAT. Richards said: 'I delivered what I said would take five years in only three, and you cannot look upon that as a down. It's very positive. The senior directors at BAT are over the moon.'

NOVEMBER 20

Formula One has never really cracked the USA and the United States Grand Prix held today in 1960 at the Riverside International Raceway in California attracted a paltry 25,000 strong crowd despite Riverside resident Dan Gurney's involvement. It was the last race of the season and Jack Brabham had already wrapped up the World Championship while Enzo Ferrari didn't even bother sending his cars to the event. Stirling Moss drove an impressive race to win from Innes Ireland to complete a Lotus 1-2. Local hero Gurney had a miserable time and had to retire on lap 18 after his car overheated.

Michael Schumacher had to make even more room in his bulging trophy cabinet on this day in 2004 when he was voted Germany's greatest sportsman of the 20th century in a national poll by television viewers. Schuey, who beat Franz Beckenbauer and Boris Becker to the award said: 'I never would have expected an honour like this. It's a total surprise.'

NOVEMBER 21

French racing driver Jacques Lafitte was born on this day in 1943 in Paris. A rather late starter, he was 31 before he drove a Formula One car. He made his debut with Frank Williams' Iso Marlboro in the 1974 German Grand Prix at the Nurburgring. When the Williams team ran out of money he dropped out of the sport but returned in 1976 when Ligier entered F1.

He became the first Frenchman driving a French car, powered by a French engine, to win a World Championship race with Ligier at the 1977 Swedish Grand Prix. He took six wins, all with Ligier before retiring in 1986. With his last race he equalled Graham Hill's record of 176 grands prix.

NOVEMBER 22

For the rest of the world the death of Ayrton Senna was a tragic and terrible accident but for the Williams team the nightmare continued for years afterwards. After a lengthy investigation by the Italian authorities, Williams technical director Patrick Head, and former designer Adrian Newey were charged with 'culpable homicide' in 1996. They fought the charges and eventually, on this day in 1999 the Court of Appeal in Bologna ruled they were not responsible for the Brazilian's death.

Senna's great rival Alain Prost was also in trouble today in 2001 when his team Prost Grand Prix went into receivership with reported debts of £19.1m. Despite branding itself as the French national F1 team, Prost was not a successful team and financial difficulties began to mount when engine supplier Peugeot quit F1 and Prost were forced to pay for Ferrari units.

NOVEMBER 23

Today in 2005 British driver Katherine Legge became the latest woman to give Formula One a try when she completed a two-day test with Minardi at Vallelunga in Italy. Despite crashing after just two laps on her first run, she put in some respectable times on the second day. Team boss Paul Stoddart said: 'She's definitely got what it takes to be a Formula One driver.'

In the entire history of F1 only one woman has ever managed a points-scoring finish. Italian driver Lella Lombardi finished sixth in the 1975 Spanish Grand Prix driving a March-Cosworth. The race did not reach full distance so Lombardi picked up just half a point.

NOVEMBER 24

One of the F1's most enduring and unlikely names finally came to an end today in 2005 when the Minardi team did its final running under that name after owner Paul Stoddart sold the team and it was renamed Toro Rosso. Fittingly, it was Stoddart who drove the final lap in a Minardi car. 'It turned out to be a more emotional experience than I expected,' he said. 'For so many years, Minardi has tried to give so much to so many. Now the team has moved on to become Squadra Toro Rosso, I wish them every success, although I know I'm not alone in thinking it will always be Minardi in the minds of so many people.'

On this day in 2006 McLaren announced Lewis Hamilton would partner Fernando Alonso at the team for 2007. The young Briton was the GP2 champion and had famously been sponsored by Ron Dennis since he was just 13 years old. Lewis said: 'To be racing in Formula One with McLaren has been the ultimate goal for me since I was very young.' Ron Dennis added: 'It's obviously going to be the biggest challenge of Lewis's career so far but it's one that we are sure he will be able to meet.'

NOVEMBER 25

Today in 2006 Alex Zanardi tested a Formula One car five years after losing both his legs in a near-fatal accident. The Italian former F1 driver took to the track in a modified BMW Sauber in Valencia. After completing four laps he said: 'I'm really, really happy. I feel like somebody cast away on an island for many years and suddenly he gets joined by a top model. When I dropped my visor, the emotions were very heavy. It was pure pleasure being back in a fantastic race car. I do understand this is about much more than just driving a race car. To put a guy with no legs in an F1 car is something very special.'

Former F1 racer Gerhard Berger left the sport again today in 2008 when he sold his 50 per cent stake in the Toro Rosso team back to Red Bull owner Dietrich Mateschitz. With Berger's help the team were transformed from perennial back-markers Minardi into a race-winning outfit in 2008.

NOVEMBER 26

The doomed Jaguar F1 team was in the news today in 2002 when Niki Lauda was sacked as team principal. He was the fourth team boss since January 2000 but little progress had been made under the Austrian's direction. Richard Parry-Jones, head of Ford's Formula One programme, tried to deny the move was a sacking. He said: 'I would not agree that Niki has failed in any way. The most important thing (in Formula One) is technical depth and Niki Lauda, for whom I have enormous respect, does not have it.'

'There was no criticism of the way I work, or whatever,' Lauda told Austrian radio. 'But what you've got to know is that in England things work differently. Britons do have their unique way of solving problems. They saw away at the legs of a chair. I am neither an engineer nor an Englishman and that's why it's easy for me to accept (being replaced).'

NOVEMBER 27

No one expected Lewis Hamilton to be so competitive in his debut year in F1, 2007. Former McLaren driver David Coulthard told the *News of the World* today in 2006 that Hamilton might struggle. 'I believe McLaren have given him his break way too soon,' Coulthard said. 'He could face a very tough time with Alonso as his teammate. Alonso may be new to McLaren but he is a double World Champion. The first person you are compared to is your teammate and if Lewis struggles alongside Alonso it could destroy his confidence.'

Two years later and Lewis was the World Champion, but he said in an interview published today in 2008 with the *Woking News & Mail* that he was not out to break Michael Schumacher's records. 'I do want to win more races and championships in Formula One. But I'm not sure I want to do what Michael Schumacher did and win all those titles,' he said.

NOVEMBER 28

The first ever motorcar race in the United States was held on this day in 1895. The horseless carriage race was organised by Herman H. Kohlstaat, the publisher of the *Chicago Times-Herald* who was keen to promote the new technology. The 54-mile course was a loop along the lakeshore from Chicago to Waukegan and back again. On race day the course was covered with six inches of snow that a horse-drawn snow plough failed to shift. Because of the snowstorm, only six of the 89 entrants made it to the start line.

Frank Duryea from Massachusetts won the race, crossing the finishing line in a time of 10 hours and 23 minutes, having travelled at an average speed of 5¼ miles per hour. Another car competing in the race had a less successful day, colliding with both a streetcar and a sleigh before having to pull out altogether.

NOVEMBER 29

Advancements in safety mean serious injuries to F1 drivers are now mercifully rare but until people like Jackie Stewart started to push forward the safety agenda fatalities among racing drivers at grands prix were not uncommon. It is ironic that Graham Hill survived an 18-season career in F1, only to be killed just months after he retired, in a plane crash on this day in 1975. A double World Champion and the only man to have won the famed triple crown of the Indianapolis 500, the Le Mans 24 Hours and the F1 World Championship, Hill was flying his own Piper Aztec aircraft when it crashed at Arkley golf course in Hertfordshire, instantly killing him. He was 46.

Also killed that day were key members of the new Embassy Hill racing team, set up by Graham in 1973. Team manager Ray Brimble, designer Andy Smallman and mechanics Terry Richards and Tony Alcock all perished, as did Hill's protégé, promising young British driver Tony Brise.

NOVEMBER 30

Christmas came early for Fernando Alonso today in 2005 when he arrived in Paris for a special event to celebrate Renault's double success of winning both World Championships. The team presented their Spanish driver with the R25 car that took him to his first drivers' title. 'I saw a big box when I arrived this evening, but to have this car at home is really a dream come true!' said the Spaniard. 'It is a fantastic present!'

Another double World Champion was getting the feel back for an F1 car today in 2006 when Mika Hakkinen returned to the cockpit of a McLaren for the first time in five years. He drove the car at the Circuit de Catalunya in Spain and finished the day three seconds off the pace-setting Luca Badoer in the Ferrari. 'Although it was great fun today I also had to do some serious work for the team,' he said.

FORMULA ONE
On This Day

DECEMBER

DECEMBER 1

Although Pedro Diniz was a paying driver for most of his F1 career he still managed to outperform more illustrious teammates on occasion including Damon Hill and Jean Alesi but by 2000 he could not find a drive. Today in 2000 it was announced that the wealthy Diniz family had invested in the Prost GP team, with Pedro taking on a management role. 'I believe in Alain and this team, and that's where I see my future,' he said. The team folded a year later.

Despite rumours that he was to be dropped, today in 2005 BMW Sauber confirmed that Jacques Villeneuve would continue to drive for the team for the 2006 season. In the end Villeneuve did not finish the season with the team after he was replaced by Robert Kubica at the Hungarian GP and decided to quit.

DECEMBER 2

Another famous name in grand prix racing was heading for the exit today in 1997 when Ken Tyrrell announced that he had sold his team to British American Racing. Tyrrell entered F1 in 1968 and won three World Championships with Jackie Stewart in the 1960s and 1970s but the team had not won a race since 1984. 'This has probably been the most difficult decision I've ever had to take,' said Tyrrell. 'It was the decision which I believe is the right one. The cost to compete in F1 has escalated dramatically and the Tyrrell racing organisation is not satisfied with being relegated to the back of the grid. Our competitive spirit is too high.' The team ran as Tyrrell for the 1998 season before it was rebranded as BAR.

Yet another team was also dealt a crushing blow from which it never recovered today in 2002 when the FIA rejected the Arrows team's entry for the 2003 season. The team, which had been in F1 since 1978 but won no races, had run up considerable debts and folded entirely shortly afterwards.

DECEMBER 3

Today in 2002 Nico Rosberg became the latest son of a former F1 star to try his hand at the wheel of an F1 car. The 17-year-old son of 1982 World Champion Keke Rosberg got his chance testing a Williams car at Barcelona after dominating the Formula BMW series, and became the youngest man ever to drive an F1 car. He said: 'The first laps were like a game with a Playstation, everything went so fast and seemed so unreal. My father had advised me not to attempt too much and just enjoy the whole experience. I think I managed to do that quite well. Now I don't want to drive anything else.' He was signed up for a full race seat with Williams in 2006.

The Hamilton-mania phenomenon continued today in 2007 when the young McLaren driver was nominated for the BBC Sports Personality of the Year award. Sadly for Lewis, just like the title race, he finished runner-up, this time to boxer Joe Calzaghe.

DECEMBER 4

He may have been outclassed by his McLaren teammate Lewis Hamilton but today in 2004 Heikki Kovalainen showed he was no pushover when he won the Race of Champions in Paris, beating David Coulthard, Sebastien Loeb and even Michael Schumacher to take victory. At the time Heikki was the Nissan World Series champion and a test driver for Renault. Not used to losing, Schumacher had his excuses ready afterwards. He said: 'It's a fun event. I was less interested in being perfectly prepared for this, because I see it as less serious.'

Perhaps hoping for some help from above, Schumacher presented the Pope with a steering wheel from one of his title-winning F2004 Ferrari cars today in 2005. The wheel bore the inscription: 'The Formula 1 World Champion's steering wheel to His Holiness Benedict XVI, Christianity's driver.'

DECEMBER 5

Michael Schumacher took his title-winning Ferrari F2004 car for a spin down the Champs-Élysées in Paris on this day in 2004. The victory parade was a charity event organised by Ferrari boss Jean Todt and also featured Felipe Massa and former Ferrari F1 drivers Rene Arnoux and Patrick Tambay.

The world of F1 was shocked today in 2008 when Honda announced they were pulling out of the sport with immediate effect. The Japanese manufacturer said it would either sell the team or close it down. Star driver Jenson Button said: 'I found out the same as everyone did on the team, so it's just as much a shock for me as for everyone else.' Eventually team principal Ross Brawn organised a management buy-out and renamed the squad Brawn GP.

DECEMBER 6

Sir Stirling Moss proved today in 2004 that anything Pele could do, he could too, when he launched a new campaign to raise awareness of erectile dysfunction and the available treatments. He said: 'I first had problems getting it up after my accident at Goodwood in 1962. Not only was the situation hugely frustrating but as a man who has always enjoyed a very active sex life, I also found it extremely embarrassing.' The problem returned in 2001 after Moss had his prostate removed, which was when he approached his doctor for help. 'I like driving racing cars but I also enjoy sex,' he added. 'My message is simple: If you have similar problems, don't be embarrassed. Go and see your doctor. All it takes is 10 minutes.'

On this day in 2005 the Toro Rosso team announced Scott Speed would be driving for the team in 2006. He became the first American to race in F1 since Michael Andretti in 1993. Sadly Speed did not live up to his name and was eventually dumped by Toro Rosso in 2007 for rising star Sebastian Vettel.

DECEMBER 7

Robert Kubica, the first Polish driver to compete in Formula One, was born today in 1984. After impressing in a test with Renault in 2005, the BMW Sauber team signed him up as a test driver for 2006 but he ended up racing for the team after Jacques Villeneuve left midway through the season.

He immediately impressed in F1, leading and then finishing third in just his third race at Monza. In 2008 Kubica took his, and BMW Sauber's first win at the Canadian Grand Prix.

DECEMBER 8

Carlos Reutemann, a Ferrari star from the 1970s, rolled back the years today in 2004 when he got behind the wheel of a modern Ferrari F1 car at the Fiorino test track. The Argentine, who won five races for the Scuderia said: 'It was an unforgettable experience. I would like to thank Ferrari for having organised this test even though it was a holiday. It was really exciting and I enjoyed myself very much! The car is impressive, especially in terms of the power from the engine. It is completely different to the car that I drove back in my day. Watching on television, Formula One today can look easy, but having tried it myself I can guarantee you that is not the case!'

Like Reutemann, Stirling Moss won many races but never won the World Championship. On this day in 2006 the Englishman was awarded an FIA Gold Medal for Motorsport. 'In my career I had numerous grand prix wins, 16 Formula One race victories and was runner-up in the World Championship four times, but this is the first FIA award that I have ever won,' Moss said. 'As such, this award means a lot to me and I am very proud to receive it.' FIA President Max Mosley said: 'There are few drivers in the history of motorsport who have been as deserving of this award as Sir Stirling.'

DECEMBER 9

British F1 fans were celebrating today in 2004 when the immediate future of the British Grand Prix was secured. After months of uncertainty and difficult negotiations it was announced that the owners of the Silverstone circuit, the British Racing Drivers' Club (BRDC), had reached an agreement with F1 boss Bernie Ecclestone to stage the race for a further five years.

Eddie Jordan, then boss of the Jordan team based across the road from the circuit was delighted, despite the fact it meant extra cost for his team. 'The teams have agreed to do the race,' he said. 'It will cost us money to do it but I think it's a justified case, not just because most of the teams are based within that area but it's important for our staff and the history of grand prix racing, so I'm overjoyed that this has happened.'

DECEMBER 10

Eddie Irvine was in a spot of bother with the law today in 2003 when an arrest warrant was issued for the Northern Irishman after he failed to turn up at Bow Street Magistrates' Court in London to answer a speeding charge. Irv was accused of exceeding the 30mph limit on a scooter at Hyde Park Corner in London, and also driving without a licence or insurance.

When he joined McLaren for 2007 Fernando Alonso said he had always wanted to drive for the team but over the course of the year he fell out with Ron Dennis and Lewis Hamilton to such an extent that he left after just one year with the Woking wonders. Today in 2007 the Spaniard announced he was returning to Renault for the 2008 season. He said: 'This is the team where I grew up as a driver in F1. Now it is time for us to begin a new chapter together.'

EDDIE IRVINE FOUND HIMSELF IN A SPOT OF BOTHER IN DECEMBER 2003

DECEMBER 11

On this day in 2003 Michael Schumacher proved he was even faster than a jet fighter when he took on a Eurofighter Typhoon plane in his Ferrari F2003-GA car, in a drag race at Grosseto airport in Italy. The race was organised to mark 100 years of manned flight and the 50th anniversary of the death of legendary Italian driver Tazio Nuvolari, who performed a similar stunt in 1931 when he raced his Alfa Romeo 8C2300 against a Caprioni 100 biplane. Schumacher won the first race over 600m before losing over the longer distances of 900m and 1200m. He then took to the wheel of an historic Alfa 8C2300 to recreate Nuvolari's race with the Caprioni.

While Schumacher was recreating history in Italy, a young driver named Ho-Pin Tung was making history in Spain on the same day when he became the first ever Chinese racer to drive a Formula One car. He got his chance to test the Williams FW24 after dominating the Formula BMW Asia series. He described the experience as 'terrifying'.

DECEMBER 12

The 1959 season was decided at the final race at Sebring, Florida on this day. Jack Brabham, Stirling Moss and Tony Brooks were all in contention. After starting well and just when he was beginning to build up a good lead, Moss went out with a broken transmission. That left Brabham in the lead but in the last few hundred metres of the race Bruce McLaren took the lead, closely followed by Maurice Trintignant. Brabham then ran out of fuel but was able to push his car over the line to finish fourth and take the title.

Also today in 1964 Jackie Stewart made his debut in an F1 car when he raced a Lotus at the non-championship Rand Grand Prix at Kyalami in South Africa. He was immediately on pace, winning the second heat to announce his arrival as a major new talent.

DECEMBER 13

Today in 1995 it was announced that the BBC had lost the rights to Formula One coverage to ITV. It was a major shock but a campaign in the British press to make sure Murray Walker stayed with the sport quickly gathered momentum. The *Daily Mirror* even set up a hotline for people to call in an effort to 'Save Our Murray'. Unbeknown to the world Murray had already signed up to work with ITV but was sworn to secrecy for the whole of 1996.

McLaren finally brought a close to the Spygate affair today in 2007 when the team unreservedly apologised to the FIA for the incident and offered to impose a moratorium on developing parts on their 2008 car that could have been inspired by Ferrari data. A statement said: 'McLaren now wishes to put these matters behind it and to move forward focusing on the 2008 season.'

DECEMBER 14

When the Indianapolis Motor Speedway first opened in 1909 the poor track surface meant the first race meeting was a disaster with multiple accidents and even five people killed. The owners needed a new surface so decided to lay bricks around the whole track. Today in 1909 the work was completed and the famous Indy Brickyard was born. Governor Thomas R Marshall of Indiana laid the final brick at the opening ceremony three days later. Today, three feet of the original brick track remains at the start/finish line.

After Fernando Alonso fell out with the McLaren team after one ill-fated season, they needed to find a replacement at short notice. Today in 2007 they announced that Finnish driver Heikki Kovalainen was to partner Lewis Hamilton for the season. The former Renault driver said: 'As a Finn it's an honour for me to follow in Mika and Kimi's footsteps.' McLaren bigwig Martin Whitmarsh said he expected Hamilton and Kovalainen to be a 'formidable combination.'

DECEMBER 15

History was made today in 2006 when Marco Andretti drove an F1 car for the first time at a test at Jerez in Spain. Marco, son of former F1 driver Michael, and grandson of legendary racer and 1978 F1 World Champion Mario Andretti became the first ever third generation F1 driver when he did 33 laps in a Honda.

Also on this day in 2006 former F1 driver Clay Regazzoni was killed in a road accident in Italy. The 67-year-old Swiss racer died in a collision with a lorry on a motorway near Parma. Regazzoni won five races in his 11-year F1 career, which ended when he was paralysed from the waist down in a crash at Long Beach in 1980. He spent five years at Ferrari and gave the Williams team their first ever F1 victory at Silverstone in 1979.

DECEMBER 16

Colin Chapman was one of the most successful and probably the most innovative team boss Formula One has ever had. Under his brilliant technical guidance Team Lotus won seven constructors' titles, six drivers' titles, and the Indianapolis 500. He was noted for his innovations and brought the first monocoque chassis to F1 with the Lotus 25 and pioneered the 'ground effect' aerodynamic designs. He was also the first team boss to bring commercial sponsorship to the sport. He died of a heart attack on this day in 1982 aged just 54.

Before the McLaren Spygate scandal broke many paddock observers had speculated that Ron Dennis would step down from his role as team principal but today in 2007 the veteran boss announced he would not be leaving. 'I'm not going to quit. That is 100 per cent,' he said. 'I know there are people out there who want me to retire, but I'm not. I do not think it would be in the best interests of the team.' He eventually left in 2009 after overseeing Lewis Hamilton win the 2008 World Championship.

DECEMBER 17

After the longest lead-in time of any team in history, Toyota Racing finally unveiled their first F1 car on this day in 2001. The Japanese team had been testing for a full year before submitting their entry for F1. Ove Andersson, then president of Toyota Motorsport said at the launch: 'Success is not a matter of money. It is about a good team working well together and getting everything right.' Seven years and a lot of money later Toyota are yet to take their first F1 win.

One of the longest relationships in F1 ended today in 2004 when Ford announced it would no longer be working with Sir Jackie Stewart, ending a 40-year association. JYS won his three F1 World Championships with Ford engines and used them again in the 1990s when he started his own team.

DECEMBER 18

The termination of the Ford/Stewart partnership was announced almost exactly eight years after the American car giant agreed to supply Stewart's new team with engines on this day in 1996. The Blue Oval had been supplying Sauber but ended this deal to go into partnership with Sir Jackie who was setting up Stewart Grand Prix with his son Paul. The team picked up one win, at the Nurburgring in 1999 with Johnny Herbert before it was rebadged as Jaguar in 2000.

Yet more changes were afoot today in 2001 at the most politically-minded team in the pitlane: BAR. After overseeing a disastrous entry into the sport in 1999 and with little progress since then, Craig Pollock, the team principal and driving force behind the creation of the team resigned under heavy pressure from the team's backers British American Tobacco. 'I am extremely proud of what has been achieved at British American Racing,' said Pollock. Under his stewardship the team had scored just 37 points in three full seasons.

DECEMBER 19

The Minardi team were the ultimate F1 survivors. Each year they went racing, living a hand-to-mouth existence and never having the funding to move up from the back of the grid. The team may not have troubled the scorers much but they did bring a lot of young drivers into the sport including Giancarlo Fisichella, Fernando Alonso, Mark Webber and Jarno Trulli. Today in 2005 Giancarlo Minardi, the man who founded the team in 1980, finally left for the last time after the squad had been sold to Red Bull and renamed Toro Rosso.

Alonso himself was also on the move on this day in 2005 when it was announced he had signed for McLaren for the 2007 season. The Renault driver was the reigning World Champion and said: 'It will be a new beginning for me and a tremendous challenge.' The switch did not seem to unsettle Alonso or the Renault team as they won both drivers' and constructors' championships in 2006.

DECEMBER 20

Faced with another season of Williams-Renault domination and knowing that his McLaren team would not have a championship-winning car for 1993 Ayrton Senna considered taking the year off as a sabbatical. Another option open to him was to follow Nigel Mansell's lead and switch to the American CART series. Today in 1992 Senna drove a Penske IndyCar at a highly secret test in Phoenix, Arizona. Egged on by close friend and double F1 World Champion Emerson Fittipaldi, who was now driving for Penske, Senna took the car around the small Firebird West circuit. He beat Fittipaldi's lap time by half a second. Nigel Beresford, head of engineering for the Penske team, remembered the day: 'He came back into the pits and said "Thank you very much, I've learned what I needed to know." Then he got out of the car and that was that.'

In the end Senna decided to stay in F1 with McLaren and he never sat in an IndyCar again.

DECEMBER 21

Many fans would argue Formula One is exciting enough in real life without being dramatised in a movie but today in 1966 saw the release of the *Grand Prix* film in the USA. Although the plot is a little on the light side, the film is fondly remembered by racing fans for including real race footage mixed in with the staged scenes. James Garner starred as Pete Aron while Phil Hill, Graham Hill, Juan Manuel Fangio, Jim Clark, Jochen Rindt and Jack Brabham are just some of the real F1 drivers with cameo roles. Adolfo Celi playing Agostini Manetta delivers the best line of the film to Garner's character: 'There are fewer than thirty men in the world qualified to drive Formula One; a mere half-dozen, perhaps, to win. At this moment, I am inclined to think you are not one of them.'

Rising star Adrian Sutil was signed by the short-lived Spyker F1 team today in 2006 for the 2007 season. A former teammate of Lewis Hamilton in the European F3 series, the young German showed flashes of his skill and remained with the team when it was renamed Force India in late 2007.

DECEMBER 22

A new team was given the go ahead to join the elite ranks of the Formula One pitlane today in 2005 when Super Aguri received the approval of all the other teams. The team had submitted a late application to race but with no objections from the other teams the new Japanese squad was ready to go.

Team boss Aguri Suzuki, a former F1 driver himself, said: 'I would like to thank all of the teams for approving our late entry and assure them that Super Aguri Formula One team will co-operate and do our best to reach your expectations.' The team ran Takuma Sato as lead driver and received engines and a lot of support from Honda.

DECEMBER 23

Russia and motor racing have never gone hand in hand. There have never been any Russian drivers, teams or races of note but in the late 1990s former Arrows boss Tom Walkinshaw was keen to change this and brokered a deal to build an F1 track in Moscow. The deal reportedly angered some of Moscow's criminal bosses who had wanted to build a casino on the site and today in 2000 Joseph Ordzhonikidze, the deputy-mayor of Moscow who had done the deal with Walkinshaw, was critically injured when gunmen sprayed more than 30 bullets into his car. He survived after a long operation but his chauffeur was killed. Police immediately focused on the F1 deal as the motive.

Today in 2004 was a much happier day for racing fans in Holland when Dutchman Christijan Albers was confirmed as a Minardi driver for the 2005 season. He was the first Dutchman to race in F1 since Jos Verstappen. He had nearly three years in the sport before he returned to the DTM series in 2007.

DECEMBER 24

John Cooper, co-founder, with his father Charles, of the Cooper Car Company, died on this day in 2000, aged 77. The two Coopers started building racing cars after the Second World War and in 1958 Stirling Moss drove a Cooper-Climax to victory in the Argentine GP, giving the firm its first win. It was the first time a rear-engined car had won in F1 and it started a revolution – within two years rear-engined designed cars made up the whole grid, but not before Jack Brabham won the World Championship and Cooper Cars took the constructors' title in 1959.

Charles Cooper died in 1964 and soon afterwards John sold the company and semi-retired to run a car dealership in Sussex. In January 2000 Cooper was awarded a CBE for his services to the automobile industry.

DECEMBER 25

Denis Jenkinson was the most famous Formula One journalist in the world and after a spirited but under funded racing career he turned to reporting when he became the grand prix correspondent for *Motorsport* magazine in 1953, writing under the name DSJ. He continued to act as a co-driver and in 1955 he won the Mille Miglia road race in Italy with Stirling Moss in a Mercedes. 'Jenks' used a series of notes about the track and obstacles – a revolutionary innovation at the time which is now standard for any rally driver. Motor racing lore has it that Jenks took to the public roads in Hampshire on Christmas Day 1958 in an unregistered, unsilenced, un-road legal Lotus Formula Two car. He reasoned the roads would be quieter and police scarce on the festive holiday.

Wilson Fittipaldi was born on Christmas Day in 1943. The elder brother of double F1 champion Emerson, Wilson never hit the heights of his brother, scoring just three points in 35 race starts.

DECEMBER 26

One of the most successful and remarkable driver/owner relationships began today in 1958 when Jim Clark met Colin Chapman for the first time. The pair were racing each other in a ten-lap race at Brands Hatch, which, surprisingly, Chapman won with Clark second. The young Scot impressed Chapman so much he gave him a run in a Lotus Formula Junior car. By 1960 Chapman had him signed up for his Lotus team and three years later Clark was World Champion.

Together Clark and Chapman dominated the sport and at the wheel of his Lotus cars Clark won two F1 World Championships, and then a record 25 grands prix, took 33 pole positions and even won the Indianapolis 500. When Clark was killed in an accident at Hockenheim in 1968 Chapman was devastated and said publicly that he had lost his best friend.

DECEMBER 27

Juan Pablo Montoya was already an extremely successful racing driver before he entered Formula One in 2001, having already won the Champ Car title in 1999 – his rookie year – and winning the Indianapolis 500 and the Daytona 24, all at the first attempt. His switch to F1 with the Williams team was much anticipated by fans and sport insiders alike. It didn't take long for him to get up to speed and he took his first victory at the 2001 Italian Grand Prix at Monza.

He was tipped for a tilt at the title in 2002 but it never materialised as Ferrari and Michael Schumacher steamrollered their way through the season, with just two races out of 17 not won by a Ferrari. Montoya took no victories at all by did get some consolation today in 2002 when he was voted Latin American Driver of the Year.

DECEMBER 28

In the early 1960s it was not uncommon for the Formula One season to finish late in December, and today in 1963 the year concluded with the South African Grand Prix at East London, a full two months after the previous round, the Mexican Grand Prix. Jim Clark had already won his first World Championship before the race but he did not ease off and after starting on pole he raced to a dominant victory, nearly a minute ahead of second-placed man Dan Gurney. It was Clark's seventh win of the ten-race season – then a new record for most wins in a season.

It was a dream season for Team Lotus boss Colin Chapman. Not only had his lead driver Jim Clark won the World Championship in record-breaking fashion but Lotus also wrapped up the constructors' title. It was a breakthrough result for the team, which went on to win another six constructors' crowns over the following 15 years.

DECEMBER 29

The South African Grand Prix at East London on this day in 1962 came a staggering three months after the previous round of the World Championship at the United States GP. It was a title showdown between Graham Hill and Jim Clark. Hill led Clark in the table by nine points but the scoring system meant that a win for Clark would hand him the title. The Scotsman took pole with Hill alongside him but in the race Hill could not keep up with Clark who looked like he would pull off the win he needed. Disaster struck on lap 62 when he got an oil leak and had to retire. Hill won the race and took his first World Championship title.

With Hill winning the race and the drivers' title his team British Racing Motors (BRM) also won the constructors' title for the first time. Like lead driver Jim Clark, rival team Lotus needed to win to take the title. This proved to be the high point for BRM: the team never won another constructors' title, finishing second in the next three seasons.

DECEMBER 30

English racing driver Guy Edwards was born on this day in 1942. He made his Formula One debut with Graham Hill's Embassy Team in 1974 but only did seven races before breaking his wrist in a Formula 5000 race. He returned with the Hesketh team in 1976 and eventually competed in 17 races, scoring no points.

He is best remembered as one of the drivers, along with Arturo Merzario, Brett Lunger and Harald Ertl, who saved Niki Lauda's life by pulling him from his burning car at the 1976 German Grand Prix at the Nurburgring. He was later awarded the Queen's Gallantry Medal for his bravery.

DECEMBER 31

Sir Malcolm Campbell, racing driver and adventurer, died on this day in 1948, aged 63. Campbell broke the land speed record nine times between 1924 and 1935 and on his last run he became the first person to drive a car at over 300 miles per hour. He also set the water speed record four times, with a highest speed of 141.740 mph in the Bluebird K4. As a grand prix driver he won both the 1927 and 1928 Grand Prix de Boulogne driving a Bugatti T39A. Despite his daredevil lifestyle he did not die in an accident, but passed away after a series of stokes. His son Donald also set speed records on both land and water, but died in 1967 when his craft Bluebird K7 flipped and disintegrated at a speed in excess of 300 mph.

One of the most influential figures in modern F1 is not a driver, designer or even a team owner. Hermann Tilke is the track architect responsible for many of the new circuits. The German has designed the Sepang Circuit in Malaysia, and the Bahrain, Shanghai, Istanbul and Valencia tracks. He was born on this day in 1954 in Germany.